The
Candlestick
Course

John Wiley & Sons

Founded in 1807, John Wiley & Sons is the oldest independent publishing company in the United States. With offices in North America, Europe, Australia and Asia, Wiley is globally committed to developing and marketing print and electronic products and services for our customers' professional and personal knowledge and understanding.

The Wiley Trading series features books by traders who have survived the market's ever-changing temperament and have prospered—some by reinventing systems, others by getting back to basics. Whether a novice trader, professional or somewhere in between, these books will provide the advice and strategies needed to prosper today and well into the future.

For a list of available titles, please visit our Web site at www.WileyFinance.com.

A MARKETPLACE BOOK

The Candlestick Course

STEVE NISON

WILEY

John Wiley & Sons, Inc.

Published by John Wiley & Sons, Inc., Hoboken, New Jersey
Published simultaneously in Canada

MetaStock Charts courtesy of Equis International

For general information on our other products and services, or technical support, please
contact our Customer Care Department within the United States at 800-762-2974,
outside the United States at 317-572-3993 or fax 317-572-4002.

Wiley also publishes its books in a variety of electronic formats. Some content that
appears in print may not be available in electronic books.

For more information about Wiley products, visit our web site at www.wiley.com.

Library of Congress Cataloging-in-Publication Data:

Nison, Steve.
    The candlestick course / Steve Nison.
        p.   cm.   — (A marketplace book)
    ISBN 0-471-22728-5 (CLOTH)
    1. Stocks—Prices—Charts diagrams, etc.   2. Investment analysis.   3. Stock price
forcasting.   4. Stocks—Prices—Japan—Charts, diagrams, etc.   I. Title.   II. Series.
    HG4638.N569 2003
    332.63'2042—dc21   2003000572

Printed in the United States of America

10 9 8 7 6 5 4 3 2 1

Contents

Foreword

Whcn I was a brand-new trader, I purchased Steve Nison's first book, *Japanese Candlestick Charting Techniques*. As I began to turn the pages, I mused, "Ah, here is a book that talks about charts in a way I can understand and enjoy!"

I'd become overwhelmed by other books on technical analysis—books that threw me into mazes of indicators and oscillators and parabolic trailing stops. Immersing myself in these tomes inevitably brought on one result . . . a nap.

Steve's book was different. In its pages, I discovered the world of candlestick charting, a technique created centuries ago by a Japanese rice trader. The history of candlesticks fascinated me, as did the picturesque names of many of the formations, names such as morning star, hanging man, and dark cloud cover. I soon learned that these patterns revealed much more than their symbolic names. They displayed the trader's most important signal— that of a price trend reversal, or change.

After having stared at cold and stoic bar charts for months, I welcomed the chance to replace them with candlesticks. I quickly adopted the popular method of assigning green and red colors to the positive and negative candles, respectively.

I soon found that these storytellers helped me assess a stock's price pattern rapidly. With the help of other indicators, candlesticks aided me in gauging a stock's possible future movement with a high degree of accuracy. I felt a debt of gratitude to Steve Nison for bringing this powerful information to the Western world.

Please realize that before *Japanese Candlestick Charting Techniques* (often referred to as the "bible of candle charting") was published in 1991, candlestick charting techniques remained deeply hidden in the East. We are fortunate that Steve Nison researched this unique charting system and brought it to Europe and the United States. His efforts literally revolutionized technical analysis of the financial markets.

As a trader or investor, your interest in candle charts will present you with many benefits. First, even if you are relatively new to technical analysis, candlestick patterns are easy and enjoyable to learn. Second, as mentioned earlier, they give you an edge on spotting possible price reversals. Next, combined with other Western indicators, they become a potent decision-support tool that can confirm or enhance buy/sell signals. Finally, the ability to read candle formations adds to your efficiency and effectiveness in reading overall markets and trends. These benefits should have a positive affect on your trading or investing account's bottom line.

Some years after I became a student of candlesticks, I attended a large trading conference held in Ontario, California. By this time, I had written my own book, *A Beginner's Guide to Day Trading Online*, and had another in process, *A Beginner's Guide to Short-Term Trading*. A glance at the conference program told me Steve Nison was speaking that afternoon. I immediately decided to attend his workshop and introduce myself to him.

I enjoyed Steve's lecture, and afterward, elbowed my way through the crowd to the podium. When I introduced myself, he shook my hand, and smiled. "Toni Turner?" he said. "Oh, yes, I know who you are. I bought your book on day trading. It's great." I returned his smile and I glowed for the remainder of the conference.

I am now honored and gratified to say that Steve Nison and I have become good friends. Among the leaders in the financial field, this wise and savvy *gentle*man is held in the highest regard. Whether he is presenting a seminar, writing a book, or teaching an online course, he is the consummate professional. I especially enjoy his jabs of dry humor, which make learning the intricacies of technical analysis pleasurable and downright fun.

This course book has been designed as an interactive study guide. A supplement to Steve Nison's books, video, and online courses, it gives you the framework in which to study and apply candlestick charting techniques. Each chapter includes learning objectives, key terms, content to study, and thought-provoking questions. You'll find the answers to the questions located at the end of each section. Please read those answers in their entirety. They contain additional information you will find useful.

I'm confident you'll find *The Candlestick Course* an enjoyable, hands-on tool you will refer to often, even after you've finished working through its contents.

As a trader or investor, acquiring knowledge and applying it properly is one of the most important steps you can take. The time you invest learning about candle charts will serve you well, and should add to your success in the financial markets.

Good luck and good trading!

Toni Turner, author of *A Beginner's Guide to Day Trading On Line*
and *A Beginner's Guide to Short-Term Trading*
www.toniturner.com

About the Author

Steve Nison, Chartered Market Technician (CMT), is President of Candlecharts.com. Mr. Nison, the very first to reveal the startling strength of candle charts to the Western world, is the leading authority on the subject. His books, *Japanese Candlestick Charting Techniques* and *Beyond Candlesticks* are known as the bibles of candlestick charts.

Mr. Nison has presented his trading strategies in 18 countries to traders from almost every financial firm, including the World Bank and the Federal Reserve. His work has been highlighted in financial media around the world, including the *Wall Street Journal, Worth* magazine, and *Barron's*. He was previously a senior technical analyst at Merrill Lynch and senior vice president at Daiwa securities. He holds an MBA in Finance and Investments.

Candlecharts.com offers a wide array of services and products that complement this workbook, including on-site and Web-based seminars, candlestick software, advisory services, and video workshops.

You are invited to sign up for Mr. Nison's free biweekly educational e-newsletter. Each newsletter details a specific trading tool or technique using real-world examples. To subscribe, please go to www.candlecharts.com.

Contact Information
Web site: www.candlecharts.com
E-mail: info@candlecharts.com
Telephone: (732) 254-8660
Fax: (732) 390-6625

Introduction

As the first to reveal Japanese candlesticks to the West, I am pleased and proud that they have now become an important analytical tool for many traders and investors. Candlestick charts, also called candle charts, are especially potent for helping to spot early reversal signals and, when utilized correctly, can help preserve capital while increasing the percentage of successful trades. Candle charts display a more detailed and accurate map of the market than bar charts do. This is because candle charts open new avenues of analysis and offer many advantages over bar charts:

1. Candle charts pictorially display the supply-demand situation by showing who is winning the battle between the bulls and the bears.

2. Like the bar chart, the candle chart shows the trend of the market, but candles add another dimension of analysis by also revealing the force (or lack of force) behind the move.

3. Bar chart techniques often take weeks to transmit a reversal signal. However, candle charts often send out clues of imminent reversals in one to three sessions. The result is that candle charts often provide the opportunity for more timely trades.

4. Because candle charts use the same data a bar chart does (that is, the open, high, low, and close), all Western technical signals used on a bar chart can easily be applied to a candle chart. Since candles offer many advantages over bar charts, using candle charts instead of bar charts is a win-win situation because you get all the trading signals used in bar charts with the earlier reversal signals generated by the candles.

For example, say you have a long stock position. A candle pattern known as dark cloud cover takes shape. In the course of only two sessions, it completes its reversal signal. At that point you'd be wise to take your gains off the table, especially if there are other confirmatory bearish signals. Others, who don't recognize the pattern, are not so fortunate. They may hold their position and eventually lose some—or all—of their profits.

Another advantage of candles relates to their effectiveness on charts on a wide spectrum of markets. Futures, bonds, currencies and equities, and any chart in which sessions include a high, low, open, and close can display candlesticks.

Candle lines and patterns also apply to any time frame. Individual and institutional investors utilize them on weekly charts, swing and intermediate-term traders study them on daily charts, and short-term and day traders examine them on intraday charts.

In addition, candles give instant pictures of market psychology. Early Japanese traders placed great faith in interpreting the emotions of market participants. In today's volatile markets, driven to extremes by the impact of sudden news and events, it's easy to see why awareness of market sentiment and collective opinion is so important.

Unlike bar charts, in which opinion is not so easily spotted, one glance at a candle chart tells you instantly how people feel about a stock or market. A candle's extended real body demonstrates definite bullish or bearish control. Conversely, a small real body indicates indecision or a tug-of-war between the bulls and bears with no apparent winner. (We discuss these aspects in Chapter Two). Both strong opinion and indecision are extremely important signals to market players, and candlesticks broadcast them quickly and efficiently.

ABOUT THE BOOK

A Japanese proverb says, "Like both wheels of a cart." This is an apt way to describe this book. The first wheel of this book provides a basic foundation for those new to candle charts or for those who want to reinforce their understanding. The second wheel consists of the many questions interspersed throughout the book. These provide a quick way to gauge the depth of your understanding and will help solidify the concepts addressed. It is the questions and interactive sections that separate this book from my others.

The Candlestick Course has two main audiences: those who are novices to candle charts and those who are knowledgeable and want to gauge their depth of understanding. It focuses on the critical aspects of candle charts that are so important for successfully harnessing their power. The goal is not to educate you on all the candle patterns and techniques but to show you how to recognize and use the more important and widely used candle signals. Most important, the book offers a way to quantify your understanding of the basic concepts and principles.

Keep in mind that the tools addressed in the course should be only a part of your analysis. If you have favorite Western tools, such as volume or moving averages, stay with them, and add the candle charting techniques to your analysis.

Each chapter contains sections that include learning goals, key terms, discussions for hands-on application, and questions. Please use the questions at the end of each section to check your understanding of the material presented. To maximize the effectiveness of this workbook, I've used a spectrum of questions, from multiple-choice to exhibits and real-world chart examples. While the questions may be short, many of the answers are lengthy so as to aid understanding. Don't skim through the answers; they are designed to be another avenue of education. The more time you spend absorbing the discussions and applying what you've learned by answering the questions, the more effective (think *profitable*) your decisions will be in the real financial world.

Chapters One, Two, and Three describe how to recognize the candle signals, how to use them to gauge if the trend is changing, and questions and answers are given at the end of each section.

Chapter Four has practical applications of the principles discussed in the earlier chapters, as well as trading guidelines.

Chapter Five is unique: We take a five-month daily chart and dissect that chart a day, or a few days, at a time.

In Chapter Six we bring it all together, with charts and related questions to provide real-world, hands-on practice.

A visual glossary of candlestick terms appears at the end of the book.

Chapters One to Three include Side Lights and Key Points. The Side Lights detail interesting facts or added information. The Key Points are answers to the questions I am most frequently asked at my seminars.

A Japanese proverb states, "The depth of the foundation determines the height of the wall." *The Candlestick Course* provides a foundation of knowledge for immediately harnessing the power of candle charts and will serve as a solid foundation for all your future work with candle charts.

CHAPTER ONE

The Essentials

SECTION ONE

Candlestick Overview: Origins and Basic Applications

T he financial markets represent some of the most exciting and challenging arenas on earth. Those who participate in these markets conduct research by utilizing two basic types of analysis: fundamental and technical. Fundamental analysts pore over fiscal statements and company reports, and technical analysts scan charts to assess a market, stock, or any other financial instrument.

Though the fundamentals are important, the shorter the time frame, the more important the psychological component of the market becomes. And the only way to measure the emotional aspect of the markets is through technical analysis. Indeed, there are many times when the emotional conditions of the market overwhelm the fundamentals. For example, how many times have we seen the appearance of a positive fundamental only to have that market descend? Even if we have a strong stock based on the fundamentals, what is likely to happen to that stock if the overall market is down sharply? Of course, the negative psychology of the overall market will influence that stock even if its fundamentals didn't change. As Bernard Baruch cogently put it, "What is important in market fluctuations are not the events themselves,

1

but the human reactions to these events." The most potent way you can gauge the emotional state of the market is through candlestick charts.

In the pages that follow, you'll learn how Japanese candlestick techniques promote efficient and effective analysis. As your proficiency in interpreting candle charts evolves, the knowledge absorbed and its application should add to your success in the financial markets. Since the terms *candlestick charts* and *candle charts* are used interchangeably in the trading community, that is how they are used throughout the book.

In this section you will learn . . .

- Background of candlestick charting techniques
- Markets and time frames in which candles are utilized
- Limitations of candle charts
- Importance of risk/reward
- Significance of using other technical tools with candle charts

Key terms to watch for:

- Reversal signals
- Candle lines
- Price targets
- Risk/reward

The use of candlestick charts originated in Japan. Since little or no currency standard existed during those times, rice represented a medium of exchange. Feudal lords would deposit it in warehouses in Osaka and sell or trade the coupon receipts whenever they chose. Therefore, rice became the first futures market.

In the 1700s, Munehisa Homma, a rice trader from a wealthy family, studied all aspects of rice trading from fundamentals, such as weather, to market

 SIDE LIGHT

Centuries ago, Japanese merchants were at the bottom of that country's social system, below soldiers, farmers, and artisans. By the 1700s, though, merchants moved up in prominence. Even today, the traditional greeting in Osaka is "Mokarimakka?" which translates to, "Are you making a profit?"

psychology. He subsequently dominated the rice markets and amassed a huge fortune. Homma's trading techniques and principles eventually evolved into the candlestick methodology used by Japanese technical analysts with the start of the Japanese stock market in the 1870s.

The greatest advantage to using candles on your charts, instead of bars, is that single candle lines and multiple candle patterns offer more reliable, earlier, and more effective reversal signals.

Reversal signals are the meat and potatoes of traders and investors. Major trend reversals represent the territory where the most gains are pocketed (and lost). In addition, the ability to identify possible reversal signals on the markets is invaluable for applying money-management strategies to improve profits and, equally important, preserve profits.

No single technical indicator, however, represents the holy grail. Like other indicators, candlesticks have limitations.

As will be detailed later, the candle line is constructed from the open, high, low, and close, which is the same data used in bar charts. Therefore, for a candle line or pattern to offer a proper signal, you must wait for the session's close to confirm it. To hasten the reading, however, rather than waiting for the end of a daily session (for a daily chart), you can look at a shorter time frame (i.e., an intraday chart) and obtain an earlier signal.

Let's say it's midday and you are focusing on a daily chart. Your view of the market is that it may be ready to rally. Rather than waiting for the end of the daily session to see if a bullish candle signal is confirming your outlook, you can switch to an hourly chart and see if any bullish candle patterns formed in the morning on the hourly chart.

Be aware that although candle signals can demarcate areas of support and resistance, they do not offer price targets. This is why it is so important to use classic Western techniques, such as pivot highs and lows, or trend lines, since these can be used to obtain a potential target. Before initiating a trade with a candle signal, always consider the risk versus the reward (risk/reward) of that trade. I repeat: NEVER PLACE A TRADE WITH A CANDLE SIGNAL UNTIL YOU HAVE CONSIDERED THE RISK/REWARD OF THE POTENTIAL TRADE. For example, if there is a bullish candle signal, such as a hammer, the risk (stop-out level) should be under the low of that hammer. Now that we have defined the risk, the next step is defining the potential target. Defining a target can be done in many ways, including a prior high or a falling resistance line. Now we have the risk/reward parameters defined, only then should you decide whether or not to place a trade. Bullish hammer or not, if the risk is $2 and the target is also $2 from the hammer's buy signal (which comes on the close of that session), this is not a trade that warrants action.

As a Japanese proverb says, "His potential is that of the fully drawn bow, his timing the release of the trigger." The timing of the release of the trigger depends on the risk/reward aspect of the trade.

Although candle lines and patterns may offer excellent signals, I advise using them in combination with other technical indicators. Just as several strands wound together are stronger than a single fiber, so is the combined power of several indicators all giving the same buy or sell signal.

Proceed by answering the following questions. Check your answers against the answers at the end of each section. Even if you know the answer to a question without hesitation, take time to read my explanation. You'll find additional information in my answers that will add to your knowledge of candles.

In the next section of this chapter, we'll cover the construction of single candle lines. The basic formations are easy to learn. We'll start by placing emphasis on the length of real bodies, whether short or long, as well as the lengths of their accompanying shadows. With a little practice, you'll soon be able to decipher the important signals candles present.

CHECK YOUR UNDERSTANDING

Questions for Chapter One, Section One: Candle Chart Overview

1. The candlestick chart was invented by

   a. the Chinese.

   b. the Japanese.

   c. no one knows.

   d. the Koreans.

2. Candle charts are believed to have started

   a. in the 1600s, in the rice futures markets.

   b. in the 1870s, with the opening of the Japanese stock market.

   c. in the U.S stock market, in the 1920s.

   d. in China, in the seventeenth century.

3. Candlestick charts can be used for which markets?

   a. Japanese stock market

   b. U.S. stock market

   c. Futures markets

   d. All of the above

4. What time frames *cannot* be used to construct a candle chart?

   a. Daily

   b. Weekly

   c. Five-minute chart

   d. Tick chart

5. A limitation of candle charts is that

   a. they only work with daily or longer-term charts.

   b. they can't be merged with Western technical analysis.

   c. they need a close to confirm a candle signal.

   d. they only work with stocks.

6. Another limitation of candle charts is that they

   a. don't give reversal signals.

   b. don't give price targets.

   c. can only be used on daily charts.

   d. can only be used on equities.

7. Why can you use Western technical analysis techniques on a candle chart?

   a. Because candlestick charts and Western technical analysis evolved at the same time.

   b. Because they both have closing prices.

   c. You can't use Western technical analysis on candle charts.

   d. Because candlestick charts and bar charts use the same data.

8. Before placing a trade based on a candle signal, one should

   a. consider the weight of other technical signals.

   b. consider the risk/reward of the trade.

   c. always look at a 5-minute chart.

   d. Both (a) and (b).

Answers for Chapter One, Section One:
Candle Chart Overview

1. **b.** The candlestick chart was invented by the Japanese. The name "candlestick" or candle chart is derived from the fact that the lines look like candles with wicks.

2. **b.** According to my research, the first candlestick charts were used when the Japanese stock market started in the 1870s. However, candlestick techniques likely evolved from earlier technical methodology that started with the Japanese rice futures market in the 1600s. Back then, traders dealt with the psychology of the market rather than specific price patterns. One author, writing in 1755, said, "When all are bearish, there is cause for concern." This is very similar to contrary opinion used today in the trading community. Even in those days, the Japanese understood the psychological aspect of the market.

3. **d.** Candle charts can be used in all markets that have an open, high, low, and close.

4. **d.** Candle charts can be used throughout the trading spectrum, from weekly to daily and intraday charting. For a weekly chart, the candle would be composed of Monday's open, the high and low of the week, and Friday's close. For a daily chart, you would use the open, high, low, and close of the session. On an intraday basis, it would be the open, high, low, and close for the chosen (i.e., hourly) time period. Since tick charts only have closes, we can't use candlesticks on them.

5. **c.** Because candle charts use the open, high, low, and close, we need to wait for the closing price to confirm the candle signal. However, a valuable technique is to look at a shorter time frame to obtain an earlier signal. For example, on a daily chart, we would have to wait for the close of the day to complete the candle line, or signal. If you shift to an intraday candle chart, you need only wait for the close of that intraday session to get the candle signal.

6. **b.** Candle charts cannot give price targets (although they can provide potential support and resistance levels). This is why it is best to combine them with Western technical signals that help provide a target. For example, a pivot high or a falling resistance line may be an upside target once a bullish candlestick signal is given.

7. **d.** Because candle charts and bar charts use the same open, low, high, and low prices, all Western technical analysis techniques can be com-

bined with candle charts. This is why candle charts replaced bar charts in the 1870s in Japan. Candle charts will likely replace bar charts in the Western world, as well. With bar charts, you receive only bar chart signals. With candle charts, you can use all Western charting techniques and you have the insights given by candle charts.

8. **d.** Although candle signals provide strong visual warnings of a potential reversal, a trader should always consider whether a trade based on a candle signal offers an attractive risk/reward aspect. A classic candle signal does not equal a good trade. The decision to place a trade should be contingent on risk/reward analysis. As the Japanese proverb states, "Weigh the situation, then move," or in the case of a poor risk/reward, "Do not move." Another important market timing aspect in determining a candle line or pattern is confirming another technical signal, such as a moving average or 50% retracement. Such an occurrence improves the chances of a market turn. Although intraday traders may look at 5-minute candle charts, in my opinion, one need not look at these before placing a trade (unless you are trading using 5-minute charts).

SECTION TWO

Candlestick Construction

A Japanese proverb states, "Without oars, you cannot cross in a boat." This section will provide the oars you need to build your foundation of candle charts. We will address the actual construction of the candle lines, which have the same components as bars: a high, low, open, and close. We will also delve into basic candle applications and begin to harness the power of candle charts.

In this section you will learn . . .

- How to identify the components of individual candle lines
- How to discern the difference between real bodies and shadows
- How to construct a candle line

Key terms to watch for:

- Real body
- White real body
- Black real body
- Upper shadow
- Lower shadow

GETTING STARTED

Technical analysts use three basic kinds of charts: line charts, bar charts, and candle charts. (Point-and-figure charts are an additional alternative, but they don't show a session's high, low, open, or closing prices.) Line charts are made up of points that usually represent the closing price of a financial instrument, connected by a single line.

Just as a bar chart uses the top and bottom of each bar to indicate high and low prices of the time frame indicated, so does a candlestick, or candle line (these two terms are interchangeable).

A single bar displays a small perpendicular line on its left to designate the opening price and another on the right to show its closing price. When using candlesticks, however, we draw in a real body to connect the opening and closing prices. This gives us a quick and complete picture of the stock's action and denotes prevailing sentiment.

The *real body*—the rectangular portion of the candle line—represents the range between the opening and closing prices. A white real body tells us that the close is higher than the open since the top of the white real body is the session's close and the bottom of the white real body is that session's open. A black (filled) real body shows that the close was lower than the open. The bottom of the black real body is the session's close, and the top of the black real body is that session's open. The session can be any time frame, from a minute to a month.

The vertical lines that extend above and below the real body are called the upper and lower shadows. The top of the upper shadow is the session's high; the bottom of the lower shadow is the session's low. The candlestick line uses the same data as a bar chart, but the color of the candlestick's real body and the length of the candle line's real body and shadows convey a

The top of the upper shadow and the bottom of the lower shadow represent the highs and lows of a session, whether the real body is black or white.

---

snapshot of who's winning the battle between the bulls and the bears. For instance, when the real body is black, that means the stock closed *below* its opening price. This gives you an instant picture of a positive or negative close. Those of us who stare at charts for hours at a time find that candlesticks are not only easy on the eyes, they also convey strong visual signals sometimes missed on bar charts.

Exhibit 1.1 shows basic candlestick formations. In (A), stock XYZ opens at 30 and closes at 35, with a high of 37 and a low of 29. In (B), XYZ opens at 35, closes at 30, and again has a high of 37 and low of 29.

Candlesticks, like bars, each represent a specified time frame. On a weekly chart, each candlestick represents one week; on a daily chart, each candlestick represents one day; and on a 15-minute intraday chart, each candlestick represents a 15-minute unit of time.

One of the most important benefits of using candles is that they give instant pictures of how traders and investors feel about a certain stock or market. A long, protracted real body translates into *very strong* opinion, either bullish or bearish. Conversely, as you will see in the chapters that follow, short real bodies mean that stock participants have no strong opinion; the bulls (buyers) hold the price up, while the bears (sellers) press it down.

Notice the long, white real body in Exhibit 1.1A. This white real body, showing the closing price multiple points *above* the opening price (in this case, 5 points), indicates extremely positive or bullish sentiment. In (B), the

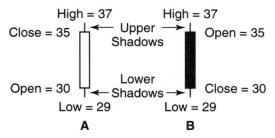

EXHIBIT 1.1 Constructing the Candlestick Line

long, black real body, with the closing price several points *below* the open, reveals negative or bearish sentiment.

The upper shadow in Exhibit 1.1a tells you that buying pressure pushed XYZ up to a high of 37. Still, while the stock closed relatively high on the session, buyers were unable to hold it at 37 into the close. The lower shadow shows that selling pressure forced the stock to a low of 29. Nonetheless, buyers came in to offer support there and propelled it up to close at 35, 6 points higher than the low.

While we're talking about open and closing prices, we know that the Japanese place great importance on these critical time periods as they pertain to the trading day. They believe, as do most Western analysts, that the first hour of trading usually sets the tone for the day. One Japanese saying states, "The first hour of the morning is the rudder of the day."

On opening, the market has absorbed and digested the events that took place since the prior day's close. The results are often volatile. The impact of market reaction can cause radical price changes for equities, or even entire industry groups. By the hour's end, the flurry of activity may subside a bit, and market participants have a point of reference with which to work.

An American market adage contends, "The amateurs open the market, and the professionals close it." Although it's an overstatement to assume the market's open is populated strictly by novices, it's true that the close of the day usually produces heavy emotional involvement. During the last hour, many market players adjust their positions. This is the time when traders, investors, and institutional managers decide whether or not to hold positions overnight. Margin calls on the futures markets are calculated by their price at the close. No wonder the last hour can produce volatile price swings fueled by strong emotions and heightened volume.

Since both the opening and closing hours can be turbulent periods, if you choose to take part, remember to use caution and discipline.

In the next section, we'll discuss one of the most critical uses of candle charts: giving you early indications that the trend may be changing. Whether a mature, extended trend, or a shorter, intermediate-term trend is in place, candle lines and patterns display powerful clues that a shift in control from bulls to bears, or vice-versa, is in process or could be imminent. For a trader, this information is crucial. For an investor, recognizing these all-important signals could make the difference between keeping hefty gains or giving them back to the market. The material you learned in this section will aid you in learning how to interpret these potent signals.

CHECK YOUR UNDERSTANDING

Review Questions for Chapter One, Section Two: Candlestick Construction

1. What is the rectangular portion of the candlestick called?

    a. Upper shadow

    b. Lower shadow

    c. Real body

    d. The wick

2. What is the thin line above the real body of the candlestick line called?

    a. Upper shadow

    b. Lower shadow

    c. Real body

    d. Lower wick

3. The upper shadow of a black candle line represents the range between the session's

    a. high and open.

    b. low and close.

    c. open and low.

    d. open and close.

4. The lower shadow of a white real body candlestick represents the range between the session's

    a. open and close.

    b. open and low.

    c. close and low.

    d. None of the above.

5. A black real body on an hourly chart means

    a. the close of this hour was under the close of the last hour.

    b. the close of this hour was lower than the open of this hour.

    c. the close of this hour was higher than the open of the last hour.

    d. the open and close of this hour were the same.

6. On a daily chart, a white real body means that today's
   a. close is higher than yesterday's close.
   b. close is higher than today's open.
   c. open is higher than yesterday's opening price.
   d. close is lower than today's open.

7. What portion of the candlestick line do you think is referred to as the "essence of the price movement"?
   a. The upper shadow
   b. The lower shadow
   c. The close
   d. The real body

8. The last hour and close of the stock market are important because
   a. this is the time when market participants, from individuals to institutions, may close out existing positions or open new ones.
   b. fund managers switch sectors
   c. traders with short positions cover them
   d. the closing bell on the floor of the NYSE is rung by a prominent person

9. Using data points in Exhibit 1.2, draw the candlestick lines.

	Open	High	Low	Close
Session 1	23	28	23	24
Session 2	30	30	24	27
Session 3	27	29	26	27
Session 4	21	26	21	26
Session 5	24	27	21	23

EXHIBIT 1.2   Data Points

10. In Exhibit 1.3, for line x, area 3 represents the
    a. close.
    b. open.
    c. low.
    d. high.

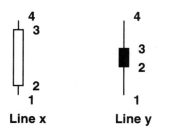

Line x   Line y

EXHIBIT 1.3   Questions 10 and 11

11. For line y in Exhibit 1.3, area 3 represents the

    a. close.

    b. open.

    c. low.

    d. high.

Answers for Chapter One, Section Two: Candlestick Construction

1. **c.** The rectangular section of the candle line is called the real body. The real body represents the range between the session's open and close. When the real body is black (i.e., filled), that means the close of the session was lower than the open. If the real body is white (i.e., empty), it shows the close was higher than the open.

2. **a.** The thin lines above and below the real body are shadows. These shadows represent the session's price extremes. The shadow above the real body is called the upper shadow, and the shadow below the real body is the lower shadow. Accordingly, the peak of the upper shadow is the high of the session, and the bottom of the lower shadow indicates the low of the session.

3. **a.** When the real body is black, it means the close of the session was lower than the open. Accordingly, the top of a black real body represents the session's open. The range between the top of a black real body and the upper shadow represents the open and high of that session, respectively.

4. **b.** If the real body is white (i.e., empty), it means the close was higher than the open. This means that the bottom of a white real body is the

open, and the lower shadow on a white candle session is the range between that session's open and low.

5. **b.** A black real body means that the session's close is under the session's open. The top of the black real body represents the open of the hour, and the bottom of that real body represents the close of the hour.

6. **b.** A white real body means that the current session's close is higher than the current session's open. In classic Japanese candlestick charting, when candle charts were hand drawn, instead of a white real body, the Japanese colored it red. However, unless one uses a color printer, the red and black real bodies would all be printed in black. This is why we have white and black real bodies, instead of red and black real bodies.

7. **d.** On Japanese charts, even an individual candle line has meaning. Therefore, one of the first clues to the vitality of the market is the size and color of the real body. To the Japanese, the real body is the essence of the price movement. This is a critical and powerful aspect of candle charts: Through the height and color of the real body, candle charts show the relative posture of the bulls and the bears.

8. **a.** The close is a time of major commitment. The closing price is used for many important calculations. Imagine a weekly chart in which the closing price above the previous week's resistance could indicate a major breakout in the offing. The close is also the time when market participants decide whether to close out existing positions, hold current ones, or open new ones.

9.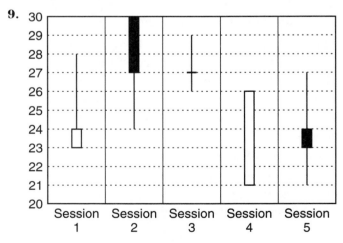

EXHIBIT 1.4 Answer to Question 9

10. **a.** A white (or empty) real body means that the close is above the opening. Consequently, the top of a white real body is the close of the session.

11. **b.** A black real body means that the close is under the open, and consequently the top of the black real body is the opening of the session.

SECTION THREE

Basic Market Strategies

Early recognition of potential trend reversals is one of the most important skills a trader/investor can cultivate. As you study candle charts and learn to recognize single candle lines and patterns, you will appreciate how candles offer an early heads up on possible trend reversals. In fact, most signals given by candle formations are reversal signals.

Candle charts often display reversal signals in a few sessions rather than over the longer time periods often needed for bar chart reversal signals. Using candle charts, you'll identify market turns quickly, which should help you to enter and exit the market with speed and accuracy.

In this section, we present the basics of trend reversals and how candles play such an important role. Also discussed are concepts inherent to trend changes and reversals: support and resistance levels and all-important breakouts and price closes above and below those levels.

In this section you will learn . . .

- How candles play a powerful role in recognizing early reversal signals
- How candle lines and patterns confirm support and resistance
- The importance of confirmation
- Why the closing price plays a key role in breaks above resistance and below support

Key terms to watch for:

- Trend reversal
- Uptrend
- Downtrend
- Consolidation
- Support and resistance

- Retracement
- Box range

The ability to recognize a potential trend reversal is one of the most important skills you can cultivate. Your ability to read candle lines and patterns will increase that skill many times over.

In the sections that follow, we'll delve into specific candle lines and patterns and the signals they give in the contexts of uptrends, downtrends and trend shifts, or reversals. At the present, however, we're going to get a top-down overview.

To start with, let's examine the anatomy of a trend reversal. A Japanese proverb states, "Darkness lies one inch ahead." You need only watch the financial television networks to see the great degree of importance traders and investors place on foretelling market tops and bottoms to arrive at an early insight on upcoming moves. As you know, the common goal is to buy low and sell high or, in the case of selling short, to sell high, buy low.

On charts, Western trend reversal patterns include double and triple tops and bottoms, key reversal days, head-and-shoulders, cup-with-handles, and island tops and bottoms.

Although market cycles of alternating uptrends and downtrends interspersed with peaks and valleys are inevitable, you should remember that trends don't always end abruptly. In fact, trends usually occur slowly, in stages, as the underlying psychology shifts.

Remember the old market saying, "The trend is your friend." Successful trading entails staying on the right side of the trend (although most find this is easier said than done). Trend change or reversal signals are the market's way of warning. It means market psychology is in transformation and you need to adjust your trading style to reflect that environment change.

For example, if you see a reversal signal, you might consider initiating a new position only if that signal is in the direction of the major trend. Say your stock has been climbing in a strong uptrend. Then, it either consolidates sideways for a few sessions or moves down (retraces) to prior support. At this time you get a bullish candle signal. Since the major trend has been up, one can use the bullish candle signal to initiate a long position. A bullish candle signal in a bear trend should be used either to cover shorts or as an alert that

![KEY POINT]

When I say a bearish or bullish reversal with the candlesticks, it does not imply that the market will reverse from down to up (in the case of a bullish reversal) or from up to down (with a bearish reversal). It just means that the market has gone from up to neutral (with a bearish candle signal) or from down to neutral (in the case of a bullish candle signal). In other words, with these reversal signals, the odds of a turn have increased but are not assured.

the market may rally and to use that rally to sell since the major trend is down.

Trend reversals or shifts are a modification in market psychology. In a strong uptrend, such as you see in Exhibit 1.5A, the bulls are in control. Shoulder-to-shoulder, optimistic bulls turn out in force, buying available supply and supporting ever-rising prices of stock XYZ. When a *retracement*, or sideways consolidation occurs (as it does from 1 to 2), the bulls stand aside, tucking their shares in their pockets. The stock rests for a time, then resumes its climb upward. Three shifts in psychology took place during each of these three movements in stock XYZ's strong uptrend.

In Exhibit 1.5B, the same bulls propelled XYZ higher with gusto. The market tops out at 3 (of course, we don't know it is a top until a few sessions later, when the stock descends). Again, those with long positions may have

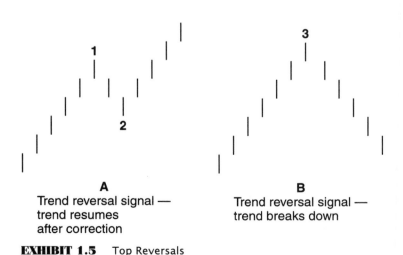

A
Trend reversal signal —
trend resumes
after correction

B
Trend reversal signal —
trend breaks down

EXHIBIT 1.5   Top Reversals

taken some or all of their profits. This time, however, the retracement turned into a trend reversal, barely stopping along the way.

Points 1, 2, and 3 in Exhibit 1.5 are reversals, and, as we don't know the extent of the move after the reversal starts, the candles will often be the first clue of a change in trend.

Besides scanning for possible trend changes, another critical component is asking, "Where are support and resistance?" Support and resistance on a chart can take multiple forms. It may be a prior high or low depicted in a price level or pattern. It may appear as a Western indicator, such as a trend line, moving average, or something as basic as the most recent high or low.

We know that a market often tops out at, or near, the same price range at which it pulled back at a previous time. It may also fall to a prior low price, then bounce off of that support level. If a candle signal confirms a support line, it would increase the potential bullish implications of that candle signal more than if that candle signal did not confirm support. Conversely, if a bearish candle signal emerges at a resistance zone, the chances of a turnaround have increased. As such, the rule is that the more technical signals—whether they are candle or Western or a combination of both—the more likely is a reversal. An example is shown in Exhibit 1.6 in which a bullish candle signal called a hammer (discussed later) confirms a support line.

In Section One of this chapter, we talked about the importance of the market's daily close. Let's take this a step further. Like most technical analysts, the Japanese place great emphasis on a security's closing price, especially if that price closes above resistance or below support. Think of it this way: If a stock, for instance, closes *above* a prior high, it means market participants are willing to pay more for it right then, *and* they are willing to hold it overnight. That means they are committed, and commitment is an extremely important factor in the movement of the financial markets. An intraday break of support or resistance does not have the same significance as a severing of support or resistance on a close.

Say you are studying a daily chart of a stock. Imagine it had moved sideways in a basing mode between $40 and $50 for the last five weeks or so.

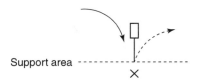

EXHIBIT 1.6   Candle Signal Confirming Support

In the context of support and resistance comes a simple and powerful technique (which, by the way, is not based on Japanese candlestick charts) that I have called the *change of polarity principle*. This concept applies perfectly to a core principle of technical analysis: Old resistance becomes new support, and old support becomes new resistance. Although this term is not generally applied to the concept, I believe it describes it well. On a chart of any time frame, you can often see how that once a markets breaks over a multitested resistance area, the prior resistance area is converted into new support. In contrast, markets that fall through prior support have trouble climbing back through it again since that previous support is frequently converted into resistance (see Exhibit 1.7).

Suddenly, the bulls wrest control of the market, and the stock closes at $53. Do you see how important that closing price is? It means people are willing to buy and hold the stock at a higher price. The market has established new demand for the stock.

Conversely, if a market trades sideways in a *box range* (as the Japanese call consolidation patterns) for some period of time, then breaks down to close below that support area, it means that buyers were unwilling to step in and hold the price at that level. The bears are in control, and that market may fall to lower prices. If, however, a session's candle broke price support by dipping below it, but then closed inside the box range, that is not as bearish. This sort of session tells you that buyers stepped in before the close, and demand was strong enough to push the price back into the prior box range by session's end.

Now you understand how valuable tool candle formations are in the context of trend reversals, along with components inherent in those reversals, support and resistance.

Old resistance becomes new support.

Prior support becomes new resistance.

EXHIBIT 1.7   Change of Polarity

In the next section, you'll learn about powerful candle lines called spinning tops and doji and how potent they can be. We'll also discuss additional in-depth market psychology as revealed by candles. Deciphering market psychology accurately is a vital part of your future success as a trader/investor.

CHECK YOUR UNDERSTANDING

Review Questions for Chapter One, Section Three: Basic Market Strategies

1. Which is most true?

   a. All candlestick signals are reversals.

   b. Most candlestick signals are reversal signals.

   c. All candlestick signals are continuation signals.

   d. Most candlestick signals are continuation signals.

2. Candle charts provide

   a. early reversal signals.

   b. hints of a false breakout.

   c. hints that the momentum may be changing.

   d. All of the above.

3. Which of the following Western technical tools can be used on a candle chart?

   a. Moving average

   b. Volume

   c. Oscillators

   d. All of the above

4. In candlestick trading, when we talk about a break of resistance on a daily chart, we mean

   a. a close above a resistance area.

   b. an intraday break above resistance by at least 1%.

   c. an intraday break above resistance by at least 3%.

   d. a close above the prior session's real body.

5. A box range in Japanese terminology is the same as a Western

   a. triangular trading range.

   b. ascending triangle.

   c. lateral trading range.

   c. bull flag.

 6. Which is false? Candle charts are best used

   a. as a stand-alone tool.

   b. on daily charts.

   c. on weekly charts.

   d. Both b and c.

Answers for Chapter One, Section Three: Basic Market Strategies

1. **b.** This is a major advantage of candle charts. They often send out reversal signals in as few as one, two, or three sessions. Some continuation signals exist, but most of the candlestick signals show bottom or top reversals.

2. **d.** Among the major advantages of candle charts is that we can use individual candle lines, or combinations of candle lines (called candlestick patterns), to obtain reversal signals in as little as one, two, or three sessions. We can also use the shape of the candle line to see if a breakout is likely to be sustainable. For example, a small real body or doji at a new high could give us a little clue that the bulls are not in complete control, and the rally may not be sustainable. We also use spinning tops to gauge whether the market's trend might be in the process of changing.

3. **d.** One of the most powerful aspects of candle charts is that because they use the same data as bar charts (i.e., the open, high, low, and close), all Western bar charting techniques (i.e., moving averages, volume, and so on) can be used on candle charts.

4. **a.** To most effectively confirm a break above resistance, I most often recommend a close above a resistance area. Conversely, to confirm a break of support, I like to see a close under a support area.

5. **c.** A box range is the same as a lateral or consolidated trading environment, in Western technicals. The name is derived from the fact that such price action resembles a box.

6. **a.** Candlestick charting tools are most potent when combined with other technical tools, such as trend lines, moving averages, and volume.

CHAPTER TWO

Single Candle Lines

SECTION ONE

Spinning Tops and High Wave Candles

In this very important chapter, we'll focus on single candle lines. (We refer to one candle as a candle line.) Section One focuses on spinning tops and high wave candles. Section Two reveals the potency of the doji. In Section Three, we'll explore bullish and bearish belt-hold lines.

Many candle signals consist of two and three candle patterns, but we can obtain volumes of valuable information from single candle lines. Don't let the simplicity of single candle lines fool you: They send compelling signals as to who is winning the battle between the bulls and bears.

In this section you will learn . . .

- Interpreting market psychology, as indicated by small real bodies and long shadows
- Identifying and distinguishing between spinning tops and high wave candles
- How to use spinning tops and high wave candles in a box range
- How to identify the hammer and the hanging man
- The importance of candle signals in the context of trends

Key terms to watch for:

- Spinning tops
- High wave candles
- Hammer
- Hanging man
- Shooting star

GETTING STARTED

Candle charts indicate early trend reversal, but they also have the advantage of displaying the force underpinning the move. Since nearly every candle line has a story to tell about the market's mood and manner, we'll start with how to use real bodies to gauge the force of the trend.

You may remember from a previous discussion that the Japanese call the candle's real body the essence of the price movement. Indeed, the length of the real bodies, in relation to their shadows, furnishes you with unique insights into the psychology of the stock market. Obviously, a tall white real body reflects a session when the bulls are dominant, whereas a black real body shows that the bears have greater control. However, when the real body shrinks (the real body can be black or white), it is a strong hint that the prior trend may be losing steam.

A *spinning top* (see Exhibit 2.1A) is the picturesque Japanese term for a candle with a small real body, either black or white. Spinning tops may have upper and lower shadows—or none at all. The important identifying trait of these candle lines is their diminutive real body. Later, you'll learn how spinning tops are components of candle formations such as morning and evening

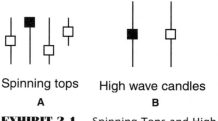

Spinning tops   High wave candles
A   B

EXHIBIT 2.1   Spinning Tops and High Wave Candles

KEY POINT

For a small real body the color is not important. The diminutive size of the real body sends out the warning signal, not the color.

---

stars, harami, hammers, and shooting stars. In Section Two, we'll talk about a spinning top that has no real body, called a doji.

A small real body shows that the bulls and bears are battling it out in a tug-of-war, with neither the bulls or bears being able to take dominant control. Selling pressure (bears) pushes the real body down, but buying pressure (bulls) keep it from being a long black real body. In the other scenario for a spinning top, demand is stepping in but supply is counterattacking and, in doing so, keeps the market from forming a tall white candle.

Spinning tops have a sort of cousin named high wave candles. *High wave candles* also have diminutive real bodies, either white or black. To qualify as a high wave, however, these candle lines must not only have small real bodies but also long upper and lower shadows. The shadows of the high wave candles need not be the same size, but both the upper and lower shadows have to be unusually long.

If spinning tops translate into indecision on the part of the bulls and bears, high wave candles indicate downright confusion. As you can see by studying Exhibit 2.1B, the long upper shadows mean that some time after the session's open, buying pressure thrust the security's price to an extended high. During the same session, selling pressure drove the price to a protracted low. Yet, by the session's close, the price returned almost to the opening price. That's confusion!

Now, take spinning tops and high wave candles into the context of an uptrend or downtrend on a chart. In a solid uptrend, a market might rise, but the shape of the candle lines during the ascent is an important clue about the sustainability of the advance. Long white real bodies are like a green light

KEY POINT

A high wave candle has the name because the Japanese compare the very extended upper and lower shadows to large ocean waves. Once again we get a sense of the pictorial representation the Japanese give to the names of the candle signals.

---

showing that the prior rally is going strongly. However, if there are small real bodies (either black or white) during an ascent, caution is warranted from the long side. This is because the small real bodies imply that the bulls have less than full control—in spite of the advancing prices. Such spinning tops are a warning not to follow this market from the long side. Spinning tops become even more consequential in a market that is becoming overextended and perhaps nearing resistance: A trend shift or reversal may be in the offing.

Conversely, if you see spinning tops moving sideways in a consolidation pattern or box range, they are not signaling a trend reversal or shift. The market is simply resting until it breaks up, or down, from that price zone. As such, spinning tops and high wave candles have no trading implications within a box range environment.

Three candle lines that contain spinning tops are the hammer, the hanging man, and the shooting star. These candle lines are shown in Exhibit 2.2. Let's first focus on the hammer and hanging man, since they have the same shape. We will then address the shooting star.

The hammer and hanging man candle lines have small real bodies (either black or white), and these real bodies have to be at or near the highs of the session. Another criterion is that they need very long lower shadows (at least two to three times the height of the real body). Because of their identical shape, you identify them depending on where they appear in an uptrend or downtrend. As you can see in Exhibit 2.2A, a hammer will appear at or near the bottom of a decline, either brief or extended; thus the name *hammer*, which suggests that the market is hammering out a base. The hanging man (see Exhibit 2.2B) has the same shape as the hammer, except that it comes after an uptrend, preferably at a new high for the move. Because of the hang-

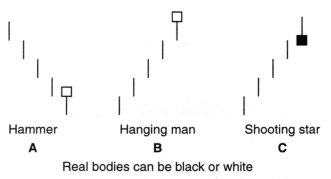

| Hammer | Hanging man | Shooting star |
| A | B | C |

Real bodies can be black or white

EXHIBIT 2.2   Hammer, Hanging Man, and Shooting Star

With the hanging man's bullish lower shadow, one might think that this line can only be bullish. Although the bullish shadow is a positive, the hanging man's small real body shows that there is some hesitation. And the long lower shadow, while it is a plus, shows that at some time during the session the market had sold off.

ing man's bullish long lower shadow one must wait for a close under the hanging man's real body before becoming bearish.

The *shooting star* is a top reversal line, just like the hanging man. A shooting star, however, displays a long upper shadow, and its small real body is at or near the lows of the session. We can see how the name describes the line, as it appears to be a shooting star, complete with long tail, soaring across the sky. The Japanese say that the shooting star shows "trouble overhead." Because of the shooting star's bearish long upper shadow, we don't need as much bearish confirmation with that line as we do with a hanging man.

As shown in Exhibit 2.2C, the shooting star is a bearish reversal signal, so it must appear during a rally. Shooting star real bodies can be either white or black.

A shooting star tells you that the market is rising in an uptrend and is perhaps becoming overbought. Finally, the bulls refuse to pay any more. The shooting star forms as the session opens near, or at, what will turn out to be the low. It rises, but the bulls cannot sustain the demand. Bears come in and

The Japanese have an all-encompassing description for candle lines that form with long lower shadows and small real bodies near the top of their range: *umbrella lines*. In one Japanese book there was a line that looked like a hammer. The text related to this figure said, "Buy from below and sell from above." As with most candlestick wisdom in the original, this text required some mental gymnastics. I finally deduced that the author meant that we should feel bullish with a hammer shape line after a falling market ("buy from below") and bearish after a rising market ("sell from above"). Deciphering these secrets of the Orient presented a real challenge!

Source: "Analysis of Stock Price in Japan." Tokyo: Nippon Technical Analysts Association, 1986, pg. 82.

drive the price back down. Remember, a long upper shadow on *any* candle means selling pressure.

As you learn and review the different candle formations, you can see how each candle line tells a story. With small real bodies indicating indecision, long real bodies showing definite opinion, and buying and selling pressure being revealed by lower and upper shadows, it's no wonder your skill at reading candle charts will add to your success as a trader or investor.

In Section Two, we'll talk about a candle similar to a shooting star, called a gravestone doji. Its appearance in the context of an extended rally is more menacing than that of a shooting star. As a matter of fact, doji in general broadcast extremely important signals.

For now, though, please proceed with the questions that follow. Don't forget to read over the answers that follow. They contain information that will add to your store of knowledge.

CHECK YOUR UNDERSTANDING

Questions for Chapter Two, Section One: Spinning Tops and High Wave Candles

1. A long lower shadow on a daily chart shows that

    a. the market pulled from its highs by the end of the day.

    b. the market bounced from its lows by the end of the day.

    c. the bulls and the bears are in balance.

    d. the bears are in control.

2. The _____ is another name for a small real body.

    a. counterattack pattern

    b. shaven head

    c. spinning top

    d. shaven bottom

3. To be considered a spinning top candlestick line, the real body has to be

    a. white.

    b. black or white.

    c. black.

    d. no color, since it's a doji.

4. What statement best defines a high wave candle?

    a. The real body must be black.

    b. The real body must be white.

    c. There must be a long upper and lower shadow.

    d. There must be a large real body.

5. What does a high wave candle imply?

    a. The market is confused.

    b. The bulls are in charge.

    c. The bears are in charge.

    d. There is complete balance between bulls and bears.

6. Which of these are essential for a hammer?

    a. A downtrend

    b. A long upper shadow

    c. A tall white candle

    d. Both a and b

7. Which statement or statements best describes a hammer?

    a. The high has to be near the close of the session.

    b. The lower shadow should be no more than one and one-half times the height of the real body.

    c. It must appear in a lateral trading range.

    d. Both b and c.

8. The color of a hammer's real body is

    a. black.

    b. white.

    c. plaid.

    d. either black or white.

9. What differentiates the hammer from the hanging man?

    a. The color of the real body.

    b. The hanging man has no upper shadow, whereas the hammer can have a long upper shadow.

    c. The trend preceding the hammer or hanging man.

    d. Hammers can be used in all time frames; the hanging man is used only for daily charts.

10. Use the following list (a. to k.) to answer the two questions marked A and B below.

   a. The market is in an uptrend.

   b. The market is in a downtrend.

   c. A long upper shadow at least two or three times the height of the real body.

   d. A long lower shadow at least two or three times the height of the real body.

   e. A black real body.

   f. A white real body.

   g. Either a black or white real body.

   h. Little or no upper shadow.

   i. Little or no lower shadow.

   j. A long, black real body.

   k. A long, white real body.

   A. From the list above, choose the four criteria needed for a hammer:

   _____

   B. From the list above, choose the four criteria needed for a shooting star:

   _____

11. Why does a hanging man need extra bearish confirmation?

   a. Because of its close near the high of the session

   b. Because of a small real body

   c. Because of its long lower shadow

   d. Both a and c

12. What does a hanging man need for confirmation?

   a. A higher high during the next session

   b. During the next session, a close under the hanging man's close

   c. During the next session, a close above the hanging man's upper shadow

   d. During the next session, an opening under the hanging man's open

13. Which candles have one-sided shadows?

   a. High wave candles

    b. Shooting stars

    c. Hammers

    d. Both b and c

14. A shooting star has a _____ real body.

    a. black

    b. white

    c. either black or white

    d. There is no real body, as the shooting star must also be a doji.

15. Pick two criteria for a shooting star:

    a. Downtrend and a long upper shadow

    b. Uptrend and long lower shadow

    c. Uptrend and long upper shadow

    d. Downtrend and long lower shadow

16. If we combine the shadows of a shooting star and a hammer, we would have a

    a. tall white candle.

    b. tall black candle.

    c. high wave candle.

    d. doji.

17. When you see a small real body at a prior price resistance area, it indicates that

    a. market participants are undecided about whether they will pay a higher price for this security; some holding long positions may choose to take profits.

    b. it's a national holiday.

    c. a continuation pattern is in force.

    d. the bulls are in control.

18. When a stock in a strong uptrend slows, and then retraces in an orderly fashion, then forms a candle with a small real body, it could mean

    a. you can take that chart off your watch list.

    b. the recent downtrend may be losing force.

    c. you should watch for the next session's possible bounce and possible long entry, as the uptrend may resume.

    d. you should enter a short position on that stock.

19. Which two candle lines have the same shape?

    a. Shooting star and hammer

    b. Hammer and shooting star

    c. Hammer and hanging man

    d. None of the above

Use Exhibit 2.3 to answer 20 and 21.

20. Exhibit 2.3 shows a series of

    a. shooting stars.

    b. hammers.

    c. high wave candles.

    c. hanging man lines.

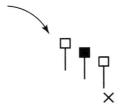

EXHIBIT 2.3   Questions 20 and 21

21. What strategy at candle line X might be best, based on this market's action?

    a. Buy, because of long lower shadows.

    b. Sell short, because of long lower shadows.

    c. Stand aside, because the trend is down but the long lower shadows show that the market bounces off its lows each session.

    d. Buy, because the last real body is white and there is a long lower shadow.

22. In Exhibit 2.4, if X is a hammer-shaped line, in which scenario would we be most likely to see an ascent after X?

    a. 1

    b. 2

    c. 3

    d. 4

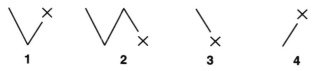

EXHIBIT 2.4   Question 22

Use Exhibit 2.5 to answer questions 23 and 24.

23. What candlestick signals are these lines?

   a. Hammers

   b. Shooting stars

   c. Hanging man lines

   d. High wave candles

24. Which line is a sell signal?

   a. None of them

   b. Line 1

   c. Line 2

   d. Line 3

EXHIBIT 2.5   Questions 23 and 24

25. In Exhibit 2.6, which of these is (are) shooting stars?

   a. 1 and 2   **c.** 1

   b. 2 and 3   **d.** 4

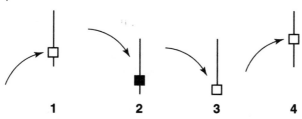

EXHIBIT 2.6   Question 25

26. In Exhibit 2.7, which of these is (are) hammers?

   a. 3

   b. 3 and 4

   c. All

   d. 1 and 2

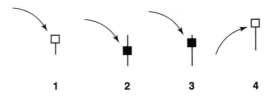

    1   2   3   4

EXHIBIT 2.7   Question 26

Answers for Chapter Two, Section One: Spinning Tops and High Wave Candles

1. **b.** Candle charts illustrate the action between the bulls and bears during that session. A long lower shadow showing on a day's candlestick means the market sold off during the session. By the end of the session, however, it bounced off the lows. This means that one of two scenarios unfolded: Either the bears retreated, or the bulls came back into the market with enough force to overcome the bears.

2. **c.** The Japanese nicknamed a diminutive real body a spinning top. A spinning top warns that the market may be losing its momentum. For instance, if the market is at, or near, a new high—especially after a steep advance—the emergence of a spinning top could be a signal that the bulls are having trouble continuing their ascent. This signal cautions that the prior move is stalling.

   One session's small real body doesn't turn the trend from down to up. Still, a series of spinning tops in the same support area shows that the bears were unable to sustain those lows into the end of the sessions. This could lay the foundation for a potential rally. The same concept would be true with a series of spinning tops at a resistance area. Such a scenario would show that each time the market climbed to that price resistance, the bulls were not able to maintain the highs into the close. This would be a warning signal to those holding long positions.

3. **b.** The spinning top (aka a small real body) is not dependent on the color of the real body nor on the length of the shadows.

4. **c.** A candle with a long upper and lower shadow is called a high wave candle.

5. **a.** A high wave candle shows that the market is in a standoff between the bulls and the bears. When a high wave candle emerges after a downtrend or an uptrend, the Japanese say the market has lost its sense of direction. This lack of market orientation means that the prior trend is in jeopardy.

6. **a.** The hammer, with its long, lower shadow and a close near or at the high, is easily understood to be a bullish signal. The term hammer derives from the fact that the market is hammering out a base. It also means that a bottom is so solid it does not break, even when a hammer knocks away at it. A hammer gives a potent signal when it appears after a significant downturn or in an oversold market. In other words, the hammer is a potential bottom reversal indicator. As such, it needs a downtrend to reverse. Since the hammer is most useful after a significant downturn, it should be noted that there may be selling on a rally from the hammer. Therefore, the first bounce after the hammer may fail, and the market may return to test the hammer's support.

7. **a.** The hammer must have a small real body at the top end of the trading range. This shows that the market initially sold off during the session, then bounced back by the session's end.

8. **d.** The color of a hammer's real body can be either black or white.

9. **c.** Three aspects differentiate the hanging man from the hammer: trend, extent of the move before the candle line, and confirmation.

10. **(A.) b, d, g, h.** The hammer can be recognized by four criteria:
    - The real body is at the upper end of the trading range. The color of the real body is not important.
    - A long lower shadow that should be at least twice the height of the real body.
    - It should have no, or a very short, upper shadow.
    - The market should be in a downtrend.

10. **(B.) a, c, g, i.** The shooting star can be recognized by four criteria:

    - The real body is at the bottom end of the trading range. The color of the real body is not important.
    - A long upper shadow that should be at least twice the height of the real body.
    - It should have no, or a very short, lower shadow.
    - The market should be in an uptrend.

11. **d.** The hanging man has a long, lower bullish shadow and a small real body at or near the top end of the trading range. As such, this candle line shows that the market sold off during the session but by the end of that session had bounced back to close at or near the highs. Although the small real body of the hanging man could give a little hint that the bulls are losing some momentum, its long lower shadow nonetheless keeps the trend pointing north. Thus, we would need bearish confirmation before turning negative on the hanging man line.

12. **b.** This confirmation is close beneath the hanging man's real body. The reason is that if the market closes lower the next day, those who bought on the close of the hanging man day (and many trades occur at the close) are now left "hanging" with a losing position. This is why I would also like to see the hanging man at an all-time high, or at least at the high in the context of a significant move. In this scenario, the longs entering on the hanging man session are in their position at new highs, thus making them more nervous. Consequently, those longs might decide to back out of their now losing position. That could cascade into more selling.

13. **d.** A one-sided shadow means that an extended shadow appears on the top or bottom of the real body. Therefore, a candle line with a long lower shadow (if it meets other criteria) is a hammer. The candle line with a long, one-sided shadow above its real body would be a shooting star.

14. **c.** The real body of the shooting star can be either black or white. Even if the shooting star had a white real body, it would still be a close near the low of the session.

15. **c.** Because the shooting star is potentially a bearish reversal signal, it must appear in the context of an uptrend. A shooting star should also have an upper shadow at least two times the height of the real body.

16. **c.** Combining a shooting star's long upper shadow and a hammer's long lower shadow above and below a short real body would produce a candle line fitting the definition of a high wave candle.

17. **a.** A small real body, whether alone or integrated into a two- or three-candle pattern, indicates indecision as to whether a higher price will be paid for this security.

18. **b.** When a stock in a strong uptrend and retraces in an orderly manner, you can watch for a small real body as a possible clue that the retracement is losing force.

19. **c.** The hammer and the hanging man have the same shape. What differentiates one from another is that for a hammer the prior trend must be down and for a hanging man, up.

20. **b.** A hammer comes after a decline and has a long lower shadow, small real body (black or white) near the top end of the trading range, and little or no upper shadow. All these lines met these criteria.

21. **c.** Although a classic hammer is a potentially bullish reversal signal, this exhibit shows us the importance of putting candles in context of the preceding price action. In this example the market is making consecutively lower lows and lower closes and lower highs. This keeps a short-term downtrend intact. However, the multiple hammers are reflecting that the market is rejecting low price levels as it descends. Consequently, the market's downtrend keeps us from buying, but the potentially bullish applications of the hammer keep us from selling. Therefore, the best strategy in this scenario would be to stand aside.

22. **b.** In scenario 2 we see a hammer confirming a prior low and therefore a potential support area. This raises the probability that the market will bounce from this area. Scenarios 1 and 4 would not be hammers, since a hammer must come after a downtrend. Scenario 3's hammer may be potentially bullish because the market is oversold, but the odds of a turn with the hammer are better with the hammer in scenario 2 that is confirming support.

23. **c.** Candlestick lines with long lower shadows and small real bodies of the top end of the trading range, during an uptrend, are hanging man lines.

24. **a.** Although these are all potentially bearish hanging man lines, the bearish confirmation of such a line comes with a close under the hanging man's real body. Since no such close occurred, we did not get any sell signals.

25. **c.** Some requisites for a shooting star include an uptrend, a small real body in an ascending trend, and little or no lower shadow. The only scenario that meets these criteria is scenario 1.

26. a. A hammer is a candle line with a long lower shadow (at least twice the height of the real body) and a small real body at the top end of a trading range, with little or no upper shadow. A hammer must also come after a downtrend. Scenario 3 meets these criteria. Scenario 1 does not have a lower shadow long enough, scenario 2 has an upper shadow that is too long, and scenario 4 comes after an uptrend instead of the necessary downtrend.

SECTION TWO

The Dangerous Doji

I n this section we'll focus on the powerful single candle line known as the doji. The doji plays an important role in candle charting techniques. When it appears in the context of an uptrend, especially in a zone of prior resistance, it can signal a significant trend shift, or reversal. Naturally, candles subsequent to the doji's appearance confirm the potential turn.

In fact, the doji's ability to convey the market's message is echoed in a letter I received from a medical doctor. He wrote, "As a physician, I can most appreciate the simplicity and effectiveness of candlestick charting. Like a stethoscope, simplistic in design, but powerful in diagnosis, candlestick charting has shown me a form of technical analysis well suited to diagnosing the health of my stocks."

In this section you will learn . . .

- The definition of a doji
- How to identify different types of doji
- The importance of doji when they appear in uptrends and downtrends
- How to interpret a doji when it forms in a box range

Key terms to watch for:

- Doji
- Dragonfly doji
- Gravestone doji
- Northern doji
- Southern doji

GETTING STARTED

The Japanese place great significance on the power of the doji. Especially in the context of a market experiencing a mature uptrend, this candle line, either alone or included in a two- or three-candle pattern, warns you that a trend shift may be in the offing.

The *doji* is a session in which the opening and closing prices are the same; therefore, it resembles a cross. Like the spinning top, the doji indicates a market in complete balance between supply and demand. Since a doji session represents a market at a juncture of indecision, it can often be an early warning that a preceding rally could be losing steam.

The ideal doji forms with the same opening and closing price, but this rule is flexible. When the opening and closing prices are only a few ticks from each other you can still consider the candle line as a doji.

Maybe you've heard the old saying, "The stock market hates uncertainty." The doji is synonymous with uncertainty. Consider the doji a warning that the framework built by the bulls may soon falter or crumble.

While doji are extremely valuable at calling market tops (especially after a long, white candle), they sometimes lose signal potential when defining market bottoms. The doji's possible negative influence at trend tops comes from its warning that the market is indecisive. As such, a close over the doji's high could be a signal that the bulls have regained a foothold.

Although a doji's appearance in a rally might signal an exhausted market, a doji's emergence in a downtrend may not portend a bottom. Other Western indicators, and certainly price environment, must confirm a market turning into a base. Why? Remember that a doji indicates indecision. Indecision and uncertainty in an oversold market may just be a resting place before another downturn resumes.

Depending on the placement of the open and close price on the session, some doji have nicknames. These doji are still reversal indicators, but they hint at more positive or negative outcomes. A few of these specially named doji are the dragonfly doji, the gravestone doji, the Northern doji, and the Southern doji. Exhibit 2.8 illustrates these special doji lines.

 KEY POINT

The pronunciation of doji is *doh' gee*. The plural of doji is doji.

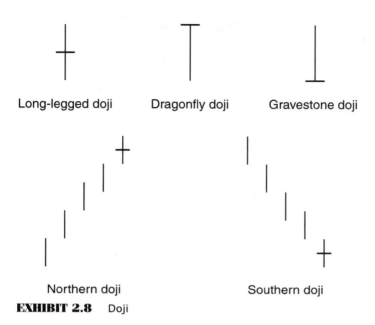

Long-legged doji   Dragonfly doji   Gravestone doji

Northern doji   Southern doji

EXHIBIT 2.8   Doji

The *dragonfly doji* forms with the open and close near, or at, the high of the candle. This candle emits bullish implications. It's long lower shadow shows that the market fell sharply during the session, but buying pressure pushed the price back up to close at, or very near, the session's high. If you're thinking this doji resembles a hammer, but without the real body, you are correct.

Pay attention when you see the dragonfly doji emerging during declines that have become oversold. Normally doji in declines are not important, but the dragonfly doji is an exception.

The bearish counterpart to the dragonfly doji is the *gravestone doji*, also shown in Exhibit 2.8. The gravestone doji's open, low, and close all reside at the bottom of the candle. From the shape of this doji you can understand its name: It looks like a tombstone.

KEY POINT

The doji is more influential when it is a rare occurrence. If numerous doji have formed on a particular chart, do not view the development of a new doji as meaningful.

SIDE LIGHT

A Japanese proverb says, "Don't climb a tree to catch a fish." The gravestone doji has an ominous sound to its name and portends a potential uptrend reversal, but don't give it more import than it has. Even though its extended upper shadow and close at the low amplifies a trend change, candle signals don't forecast the scope of a possible decline. Remember, candle signals give you early reversal or change signals, but they don't predict future price targets. So, even if there are numerous gravestone doji, it doesn't perforce mean the market will fall that much steeper. It just means that the odds of a turn are greater than they would be with one gravestone doji.

The gravestone doji's strong point is in calling top reversals. Imagine an uptrend becoming overbought, rising on white real bodies. Perhaps a glance at the chart tells you that recent resistance at this same price level is also in place. Now, the gravestone doji appears. The market opens, rises to a much higher price (shown by the extended upper shadow), then falls to the low of the session to close. For the moment, at least, the bears have won control. If the next candle falls to the downside, the signal is complete.

Naturally, if the candle that forms after a gravestone doji rises above it and culminates in a long white real body, or other positive candle line, the potential trend reversal signal given by the gravestone doji is negated.

To differentiate between doji appearing in a rally and those materializing in a decline, I refer to the former as *Northern doji* and the latter as *Southern doji*. A doji with long upper and lower shadows is called a *long-legged doji*.

Like a pivotal word in a sentence, the doji gives optimum signals when taken in the context of a prior trend, when they confirm other technical indicators or patterns, and during consideration of follow-through action.

 KEY POINT

When the market is rising and overbought, and then a doji appears after a tall, white candle, the Japanese say that the market is tired. What an appropriate way to view doji. A doji's emergence may not foretell an immediate price reversal. It may only suggest that the market is vulnerable and susceptible to change. A trader can use the highest high between the doji and the prior candle as resistance. If the market closes above that area, the Japanese say the bulls are refreshed.

In Section Three, we'll finish our discussion of single candle lines by exploring the messages displayed by bullish and bearish belt-holds and their long real bodies. We'll also talk about the psychology that underpins these candle lines "with an attitude."

CHECK YOUR UNDERSTANDING

Questions for Chapter Two, Section Two:
The Dangerous Doji

1. A doji is a session

   a. in which the open and close are the same.

   b. that creates a candle line with only an upper shadow.

   c. in which the open and the low are the same.

   d. that develops a candle with a very long lower shadow.

2. What does a doji signal?

   a. The market action is one-sided.

   b. The bears have taken control.

   c. The bulls and bears are in a stalemate.

   d. The bulls are in control.

3. If a spinning top has a very small real body, it has the same implications as a

   a. doji.

   b. long, black real body.

   c. long, white real body.

   d. None of the above.

4. For a dragonfly doji, the _____ represents the open, high, and close.

   a. low of the session

   b. middle of the session

   c. high of the session

   d. midway point of the real body

5. The doji in a rally is _____ a sell signal.

   a. sometimes

   b. always

c. never

d. None of the above

6. For a gravestone doji, the _____ is the open, low, and close.

   a. low of the session

   b. middle of the session

   c. upper 10% of the session

   d. midway point of the real body

7. As a hammer's real body gets smaller, it will ultimately become a(n)

   a. dragonfly doji.

   b. inverted hammer.

   c. gravestone doji.

   d. hanging man.

8. As a shooting star's real body gets smaller and smaller, it will ultimately become

   a. a dragonfly doji.

   b. a hammer.

   c. a gravestone doji.

   d. None of the above.

9. A spinning top is to a long real body as a(n) _____ is to a spinning top.

   a. inverted hammer

   b. bullish belt-hold line

   c. bearish belt-hold line

   d. doji

10. A doji in an uptrend is called a

    a. gravestone doji.

    b. dragonfly doji.

    c. Southern doji.

    d. Northern doji.

11. Northern doji are most effective when

    a. the doji is in the middle of a trading range.

    b. the market is very overbought.

   c. the doji appears at a resistance area.

   d. Both b and c

12. Use Exhibit 2.9 to answer the following questions by filling in the blanks:

   (A) Which is a gravestone doji? _____

   (B) Which is a long-legged doji? _____

   (C) Which is a dragonfly doji? _____

1   **2**   **3**

EXHIBIT 2.9   Question 12

13. Exhibit 2.10 shows a doji in a downtrend. Should you pay attention to this doji?

   a. Yes, because the doji is confirming a support level.

   b. No, because doji in downtrends are not important.

   c. No, because the doji works best in neutral trading environments.

   d. Yes, because doji work well in short-term downtrends.

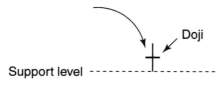

EXHIBIT 2.10   Question 13

14. Exhibit 2.11 shows doji following a tall white candle. Assuming this is a daily chart, at what price would the market have to get above to be considered a bullish breakout?

   a. A close over 2

   b. A close over 3

   c. An intraday move over 3

   d. A close over 4

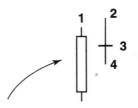

EXHIBIT 2.11   Question 14

15. Match the patterns shown in Exhibit 2.12 with their candlestick terms.

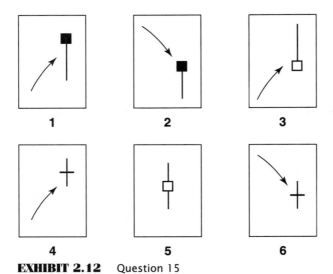

EXHIBIT 2.12   Question 15

Candlestick Name	Figure Number
a. Hanging man	_____
b. Shooting star	_____
c. High wave candle	_____
d. Hammer	_____
e. Northern doji	_____
f. Southern doji	_____

Answers for Chapter Two, Section Two: The Dangerous Doji

1. a. The doji reflects a market in a state of transition and is, consequently, one of the more important individual candle lines. A doji session has a horizontal line instead of a real body, because a doji is formed when the session's open and close are the same. Stay especially cautious when you see a doji materialize after a tall white candle in the context of a significant uptrend. This is true whether the doji is within the prior long white real body or above it. A doji means that the bulls are failing to sustain the upside drive. In this scenario, the market is considered tired by the Japanese, hence susceptible to a correction.

2. **c.** A doji is synonymous with indecision. In such conditions, the market becomes vulnerable to correction. Doji often work better as markers of top reversals than bottom reversals.

3. **a.** Although the ideal doji has the opening and closing at the same level, if the real body is small enough, it has the same implications as a doji. How do you decide whether a near-doji day (i.e., the open and close are very close, but not exactly the same) should be considered a doji? One method I recommend is to compare a near-doji day to recent action. If there are a series of very small real bodies, I would not view the near-doji day as significant, since so many recent periods had small real bodies or doji.

4. **c.** The dragonfly doji completes its formation with the open, high, and close all at the session's high. As such, it might have more bullish implications than a regular doji. The long lower shadow of the dragonfly doji illustrates the market selling off steeply during the session and then springing back to close at the highs of that session.

5. **a.** A doji is more effective if it appears in an extended rally or uptrend, especially if the market is overbought (meaning it has moved up too far, too fast). Its signal is even more powerful if it appears at a resistance level.

6. **a.** The gravestone doji completes its formation with the open, low, and close all at the session's low. Therefore, it has slightly more bearish implications than a regular doji. As its name implies, this doji sets a negative tone with its long, upper shadow. It tells you that the market opened, then moved up to an intrasession high, but fell to close at the opening price.

7. **a.** As a hammer's real body becomes smaller, it may become a dragonfly doji, since such a doji displays the open, high, and close at the high of the session. Consequently, with a hammer's small real body at the top end of the trading range, when the real body gets smaller and smaller (meaning the open and close get closer to one another), the trend culminates in the formation of a dragonfly doji.

8. **c.** The gravestone doji has the open, low, and close at the low of the session. A shooting star, with its real body near the bottom end of the trading range, would become a gravestone doji as its real body shrinks.

9. **d.** In this question, we're comparing the size of the real bodies. Consequently, a spinning top has a smaller real body than a long real body. Continuing this analogy, a doji session has a smaller real body than a spinning top session. Remember, a spinning top is the nickname for a small real body.

10. **d.** As opposed to a doji in a descending market (a Southern doji), a doji in an ascending market is called a Northern doji. In my experience, Northern doji are more effective at calling top reversals than Southern doji are at calling bottom reversals.

11. **d.** When a doji appears in the middle of the trading range, I suggest you ignore it. Doji, like most candlestick signals, are reversal indicators; therefore, they need a trend to reverse. If the market is in a lateral (i.e., box range), there is no trend to reverse; the doji would not be a signal to place a trade. The odds of a turn for a Northern doji are enhanced if the market is overextended and is near resistance. It's important to remember that the more signals you have confirming the same support or resistance level, the more likely a reversal is. Consequently, if a doji appears to confirm a resistance area, the odds of a turn is higher than if no prior resistance is in place. This underscores the critical aspect of always considering candle signals in the context of recent price pattern history. In this instance, if the market moved in a lateral range before the doji appeared, we would not use it as a trading signal. But if a doji developed after a rally, and especially if the doji confirmed a prior resistance area, it has a high probability of being a reversal signal.

12 **(A).** **2.** The gravestone doji has the open, low, and close of the bottom end of the trading range and a long upper shadow.

12 **(B).** **1.** A long-legged doji has very long upper lower shadows. It's also sometimes called a high wave doji.

12 **(C).** **3.** A dragonfly doji has the open, high, and close at the high of the session. It's probably called a dragonfly since it resembles the insect of that name, with very long wings at the top of its body.

13. **a.** Normally a doji in a downtrend (a Southern doji) doesn't work as well as a Northern doji. However, all candle signals must be observed in the context of the overall market picture. In this example the doji is con-

firming potential support. As such, this doji takes on more significance and should be heeded.

14. **a.** Since the high of the doji is at 2, we use a close above that level on which a bullish breakout would be signaled.

15. **a.** 1

    b. 3

    c. 5

    d. 2

    e. 4

    f. 6

SECTION THREE

Long Real Bodies, the Consummate Storytellers

I n previous sections, we focused on single candle lines that incorporate small real bodies. These small real bodies project indecision on the part of market participants, especially when they form at support and resistance areas.

Now, we'll switch gears and talk about long real bodies. Candle lines with extended real bodies can also display strong signals, especially when they touch support and resistance zones. Toward the end of this section, we'll summarize market psychology as it pertains to single candle lines and their shadows, as well as their real bodies.

In this section you will learn . . .

- Market sentiment that underpins long white or black real bodies
- Bullish and bearish belt-holds, what they look like, and what they mean
- The importance of belt-hold lines when they develop at support and resistance areas
- How belt-hold lines add to your money management skills
- The significance of upper and lower shadows on all candle lines

Key terms to watch for:

- Bullish belt-hold
- Bearish belt-hold
- White opening shaven bottom
- Black opening shaven top
- Belt-hold candle line
- Blow-off

GETTING STARTED

A candle chart displaying small real bodies at the culmination of an uptrend or downtrend—or even intermediate moves to the upside or downside—indicates that bulls and bears are fighting in a dead heat. The flip side of these small-bodied candle line reversals, which include spinning tops, high wave candles, and doji, are single candle lines incorporating long black or white real bodies. The Japanese refer to the candle line featuring this extended real body as a belt-hold.

As Exhibit 2.13 illustrates, the *bullish belt-hold* is a tall, white candle that opens on (or very near) the low of the session and closes at, or near, the high of the session. When it appears in a decline, it forecasts a potential rally. When it appears during an ascent, it keeps the bull trend intact.

 S I D E   L I G H T

The Japanese name for the belt-hold is derived from the sumo wrestling term, *yorikiri*. Yorikiri means "pushing your opponent out of the ring while holding onto his belt."

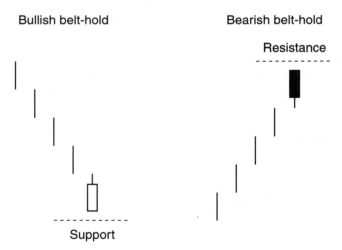

Bullish belt-hold   Bearish belt-hold

EXHIBIT 2.13   Belt-Hold Lines

The Japanese say, "A single arrow is easily broken, but not ten in a bundle." So it is with volume and candles. Volume is a significant component of market psychology. Strong volume fuels a security's move to the upside or downside and even helps to confirm trends. Conversely, a security's move up or down on low volume will often fail, as investor conviction is lacking.

A bearish belt-hold has significant power in foretelling a trend reversal if it opens near resistance, then falls to close at or near the close many points down, fed by strong volume. Conversely, a bullish belt-hold that rises off support on strong volume has more fuel to initiate an uptrend if it forms on high volume and closes at or near the high of the session.

As you can see in Exhibit 2.13, the *bearish belt-hold* is a long, black candle that opens at, or near, the high of the session, then tumbles lower as the session unfolds. If this candle line appears in the context of a mature uptrend, it may form a top reversal.

Generally speaking, the longer the height of the belt-hold candle line, the more important is the signal it gives. That makes sense, because an extended range culminating in a session's closing at the opposite end from the opening means that either the bulls or the bears dominate that session.

As you can see by the support and resistance lines in Exhibit 2.13, belt-hold lines that appear at prior support or resistance areas, thereby confirming the strength of those areas, are extremely valuable signals since they increase the chances of a reversal. Belt-hold lines also gain value as a reversal signal when they have not appeared regularly on the chart's recent time frame.

Like many candle trend reversal signals, bullish and bearish belt-holds can play an important role in sound money-management principles. Say you are long and your stock rises nicely in an uptrend. Soon, a doji or spinning top appears, then a bearish belt-hold forms. The doji was a warning to scale back on longs, but the bearish belt-hold completely confirms the reversal and could signal a time to consider closing your entire position and taking profits.

The reverse scenario occurs if you are holding a short position in the context of a downtrend. Perhaps the decline slows, and a bullish belt-hold forms at a prior support area. You may choose to cover part or all of your position, thus preserving your gains.

KEY POINT

While we are on the subject of shadows, trend lines drawn on a candlestick chart are drawn the same way as they are on a bar chart—by connecting a session's lows for a support line and the session's highs for a resistance line. There the top of the upper shadow and bottom of the lower shadow are the areas used for trend lines.

We've explored the size of real bodies thoroughly in previous pages. Still, the candle's upper and lower shadows—or lack of them—also tell a story. In the last section, we looked at the long lower shadows of hammers and the long upper shadows created by shooting stars. The long lower shadow of the hammer echoed the fact that at some time during the session the market had sold off sharply, but by session's end the market had regained all the lost ground and closed at or near the high of the session. In other words, the long lower shadow visually shows that the market had rejected lower price levels. A long upper shadow, such as that in a shooting star, illustrates a market that tests and then rejects higher prices.

Likewise, if there is a tall white candle that also has an extended upper shadow, that upper shadow offsets some of the bullish implications of the tall white candle. Conversely, the bearish implications of a long black candle are mitigated by a long lower shadow. Consequently, when analyzing candle lines, one should consider both the real bodies and shadows.

Conversely, imagine you see a market stabilizing at prior lows or a support zone, then stabilize. At that time, many of the shadows develop with definable long, lower bullish shadows—despite the size of the real body. That tells you that buyers are accumulating each time the price comes down to that support level. As a trader or investor, you might monitor that stock for a possible basing move and subsequent long entry, if and when it penetrates resistance on strong volume.

You've learned how powerful single candle lines can be. When they develop near support or resistance, they can become even more potent.

In the next chapter, we'll study candle patterns. These patterns, constructed of two or more candle lines, give incredibly powerful signals that help foretell trend reversals. Like their single candle line colleagues, patterns come with highly descriptive names, including dark cloud cover, tweezers, and three white soldiers.

CHECK YOUR UNDERSTANDING

Questions for Chapter Two, Section Three: Long Real Bodies, the Consummate Storytellers

1. What is a bullish belt-hold line?

   a. A tall, white candle with a long upper shadow

   b. A tall, white candle with a long lower shadow

   c. A tall, white candle with the same open and close

   d. A tall, white candle that opens near the low of the session and closes at or near the high of the session

2. What is a bearish belt-hold line?

   a. A long, black real body that opens at the high of the session and closes at or near the low of the session

   b. A long, black candle with a longer upper shadow

   c. A long, black candle that plunges below the prior box range

   d. A long, black real body that closes below the prior candle's low

3. When does a bearish belt-hold line become more significant?

   a. When the major trend is sideways

   b. When the major trend is up

   c. When the belt-hold is near resistance

   d. When the belt-hold is near support

4. The longer the height of the belt-hold candle line, the _____ the signal it gives.

   a. less important

   b. more important

   c. later

   d. less consistent

5. On a candlestick chart, what points do we use to draw a support line?

   a. From the bottom of the real bodies

   b. From the top of the real bodies

    c. From the bottom of the lower shadows

    d. From the top of the upper shadows

6. The smaller the real body, the

    a. greater the force behind the move.

    b. more the market has bounced off its lows.

    c. more the market has sold off its highs.

    d. less the force behind the move.

7. Imagine you held 500 shares of XYZ as a short position. The stock moved down in a sharp decline, until it neared the same price zone as the most recent low. At that support point, it rallied, forming a bullish belt-hold. This candle formation suggests that you should

    a. cover at least part, of your short position.

    b. add to your short position.

    c. wait for the S&P 500 to make a new high.

    d. buy puts to hedge your position.

8. A series of long lower shadows as the market is descending

    a. strengthens the outlook for a bearish scenario.

    b. shows that demand is easily overcoming supply.

    c. shows that the market is descending reluctantly.

    d. None of the above.

9. When analyzing a single candle line, one should consider

    a. only the real body.

    b. the upper and lower shadows.

    c. the real body and shadows.

    d. the real body and the upper shadow.

10. In Exhibit 2.14, what is the market telling us?

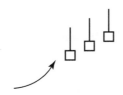

EXHIBIT 2.14   Question 10

a. The trend is fully up, as shown by higher highs.

b. The trend is slightly lower, due to higher lows.

c. The trend is neutral.

d. The trend is mostly higher, but caution is warranted due to long upper shadows.

Answers for Chapter Two, Section Three: Long Real Bodies, the Consummate Storytellers

1. **d.** A bullish belt-hold line is a tall white candle that has very little or no lower shadow and little or no upper shadow.

2. **a.** A bearish belt-hold line is a long, black real body that opens at the high of the session and closes at or near the low of the session. It has small or nonexistent upper or lower shadows.

3. **c.** A bearish belt-hold line displays added bearishness when it confirms a resistance area by opening near resistance, then plunging lower into the close. This indicates heavy supply at the resistance zone.

4. **b.** Generally speaking, the wider the price range of the belt-hold candle line, the more important the signal it gives.

5. **c.** In candlestick charting, we draw support or resistance lines the same way we draw it on a bar chart. Consequently, when we draw a support line, we connect the lows of the lower shadows on the candle chart, just as we would connect the lows on a bar chart. This brings out an important point about candle charts: Because they use the same data as a bar chart, we use the same techniques on a candle chart as we do on a bar chart, including an indicator as basic as a trend line.

6. **d.** One of the major attributes of candle charts is that they serve as a quick visual clue telling you whether the bulls or bears are in control of the market. When you see a tall, white candle, the bulls are in charge. When a tall, black real body forms, the bears are in charge. A spinning top (small real body), however, suggests the market is undecided and tells us the prior trend may be losing some momentum.

7. **a.** When you are holding a short position and wish to retain your profits, consider covering all or part of your short position when a bullish belt-hold appears at support.

8. **c.** A tall lower shadow shows that the market is rejecting the lower prices of the session. A series of long lower shadow candles, even

though the market may be falling, signals that the bears do not have full control.

9. **c.** The real body is called the essence of the price movement because of all the information it provides about the demand-supply situation, but shadows are also an important aspect. For example, a tall white candle without an upper shadow could be viewed as more positive than a tall white candle line with an extended upper shadow.

10. **d.** Although the market is ascending, as shown by higher highs and higher lows and higher closes, the consecutive long upper shadows tell us that the bulls cannot hold onto control into the close of the session. This should make one more cautious about following a fully bullish stance.

CHAPTER THREE

The Power of Candle Patterns

SECTION ONE

Close Cousins: Piercing, Dark Cloud Covers, Engulfing, and Counterattacks

Candle charts are most powerful when two or more candle lines combine in a candle pattern. Just as the Japanese endowed single candle lines with imaginative names, they also bestowed colorful descriptions on candle patterns. These descriptive monikers underscore the nature of the pattern's signals. For example, *dark cloud cover* is a bearish signal consisting of a two-candle pattern that indicates a top reversal. Of course, when dark clouds cover the sky, it is the warning before the storm.

In this unit, we'll discuss patterns that include two or three candle lines. We'll also discuss windows, which the Japanese call disjointed candles.

The section that follows explains dark cloud covers and engulfing, piercing, and counterattack patterns. Readily recognizable on charts, these candle patterns offer potent signals of possible trend changes and reversals. Use them in conjunction with Western indicators to find buy/sell setups and incorporate them into your money-management tactics.

In this section you will learn . . .

- An overview of multiple candle patterns
- How to recognize the bullish piercing pattern
- How to recognize the dark cloud cover pattern
- The importance of bullish and bearish engulfing patterns
- How bullish and bearish counterattack patterns can lead to quick trend changes

Key terms to watch for:

- Bullish piercing pattern
- Dark cloud cover
- Bullish engulfing pattern
- Bearish engulfing pattern
- Bullish counterattack pattern
- Bearish counterattack pattern

GETTING STARTED

In earlier units, we learned about the power of single candle lines. Now we'll discuss why multiple candle patterns display even more intense signals.

Just as individual candle lines send important signals about the market's health, two- and three-candle patterns that emerge during uptrends and downtrends often presage a trend reversal, or change. Typically, a two-candle pattern begins with the topping or bottoming candle; the next candle confirms the reversal. A three-candle pattern may start with the formation of a candle in the context of a trend, followed by the topping or bottoming candle. The third candle's appearance verifies the reversal signal.

First, we'll discuss the two-candle pattern referred to as the *bullish piercing pattern* (Exhibit 3.1A), which appears in the context of a decline, or downtrend. Naturally, the more oversold the decline, the more significant the signal may be. The bullish piercing pattern consists of a black body forming in the downtrend; the next real body culminates in a white real body that closes within the prior black body, preferably more than one-half of the black body's length. The white real body "pierces" the recent downtrend, with the bulls overwhelming the bears. Subsequent price action should confirm this pattern.

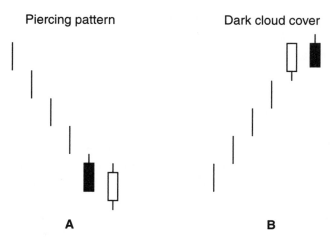

Piercing pattern   Dark cloud cover

A   B

EXHIBIT 3.1   Piercing Pattern and Dark Cloud Cover

You might expect the counterpart to the bullish piercing pattern to be called a bearish piercing pattern. However, the opposite pattern is a powerful top reversal pattern known as *dark cloud cover*.

As illustrated in Exhibit 3.1B, a *dark cloud cover* forms a top reversal pattern. The first session should be a strong, white real body. The second session's price opens over the prior session's high (or above the prior session's close). By the end of the second session, it closes near the low of the session. The black candle should ideally close below the center of the prior white candle.

This foreboding pattern graphically indicates that the bears constrained the bulls. If the black real body does not close below the halfway point of the prior white candle, consider waiting for bearish confirmation on the following session. This could be a lower close on the next session.

 SIDE LIGHT

If you're waiting for a good shorting setup, pay attention when a security in a steep uptrend that's overbought gets to a resistance area and forms dark cloud cover. When that scenario takes place, especially with high volume, you may wish to survey your other technical indicators to see if a shorting setup is at hand. Of course, a close over the highs of the dark cloud cover would be a reason to exit any shorts. Remember the concepts of stops!

Here's an example of how candle patterns add to your money-management skills by giving early warning of trend change. If you were holding a long position of a security in an uptrend and you saw the strong, white real body of the first candle soaring into the uptrend, you would surely remain bullish. On the next session, the security opens at a new high, confirming your bullishness. By the end of that session, however, the price has fallen well within the prior session's real body, indicating that the new price high failed to hold: Supply overcame demand. At this point, your bullishness may change to caution, and wisdom tells you to take profits. This is a prime example of how candle signals offer early reversal information and can aid you in locking in profits.

Next, we'll look at the two-candle pattern called the *bullish engulfing pattern*, illustrated in Exhibit 3.2. Like a piercing pattern, the bullish engulfing pattern typically appears at the culmination of a decline or a downtrend (see Exhibit 3.2A). The market falls, and a black candle forms. Next, a candle line develops with a real body that wraps around the prior session's black body. (The Japanese sometimes refer to this as a hugging line, for obvious reasons.) As the white real body opens under the prior black real body's close and closes above that session's open, it shows that buying pressure has overpowered selling pressure (i.e, the bulls have taken charge!) If the market is solid, the lows of the bullish engulfing pattern should be support. Thus, for those who are long based on this pattern, there should be a stop under the lows of this pattern.

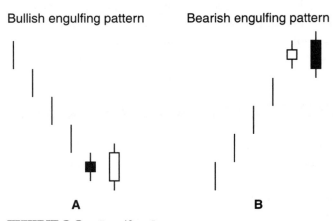

Bullish engulfing pattern Bearish engulfing pattern

A B

EXHIBIT 3.2 Engulfing Patterns

When you see a bullish or bearish engulfing pattern, you may think it resembles a Western key reversal, or outside day. You are right on the money! In classic Western technical analysis, a key reversal day or outside day takes place when a security makes a new high in the context of an uptrend. It then falls to close below the prior day's close, resulting in a bearish signal. The reverse is true for a downtrend, with the key reversal day making a new low, then closing above the prior session's open.

The flip side of a bullish engulfing pattern is the *bearish engulfing pattern*, which appears at the top of a market experiencing an uptrend. A white real body is engulfed by a black real body, suggesting a top reversal. As you can see in Exhibit 3.2B, the black real body gaps open above the prior white real body's close. Then the market falls to close below the prior session's open—a bearish signal. That movement indicates that supply has overpowered demand. Obviously, the bears have wrested control from the bulls. If the market is weak, the high of the bearish engulfing pattern should be a resistance area.

The next patterns we'll study are counterattack lines. Counterattack lines are formed when opposite-colored candles have the same close.

The *bullish counterattack line* occurs during a decline. As illustrated in Exhibit 3.3A, the initial candle in this pattern is usually a black candle. The

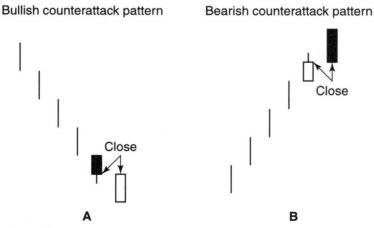

Bullish counterattack pattern   Bearish counterattack pattern

Close

Close

A   B

EXHIBIT 3.3   Counterattack Patterns

KEY POINT

With the bullish and bearish engulfing patterns, only the prior real body needs to be engulfed. Shadows need not be engulfed.

next candle opens lower, which delights the bears. Suddenly, the bulls stage a counterattack by propelling prices to the prior candle's close. This causes the downtrend to stall.

The bullish counterattack pattern is similar to the bullish piercing pattern. The difference is that the bullish counterattack line does not move up into the prior candle's real body. Instead, it returns to the prior candle's close. The inability of the bullish counterattack formation to push into the former candle's real body tells you that it may not be quite as potent as the piercing pattern, nonetheless, the counterattack line should be respected. It shows a changing of the guard from bears to bulls, and that's always a significant event.

In a *bearish counterattack pattern* (see Exhibit 3.3B), the first white candle shows the bulls happily in control. The next candle gaps open higher, but the bears rush in to force the closing price down to the prior session's close. The surprised bulls have no doubt swallowed their recent optimism and now find themselves on shaky ground.

As you've probably surmised, the bearish counterattack pattern is similar to dark cloud cover, but again, the black counterattack candle does not penetrate the prior session's real body. Instead, it closes at the prior session's close. This suggests that dark cloud cover may display a slightly stronger signal, but again, whenever supply overwhelms demand, it significantly changes the market's texture.

Bearish counterattack lines send especially potent signals when the second session gaps open *much* higher than the previous session. This tells you that the market moved strongly in the direction of the prevailing trend, then made a sharp U-turn to close at the prior day's closing price. In other words, it shot up, only to end back down where it started.

You can imagine the same scenario, with directions reversed, for the bullish counterattack pattern.

Now you can see why the two-candle bullish and bearish engulfing pattern, bullish piercing pattern, dark cloud cover, and bullish and bearish counterattack patterns are such powerful indicators. Strong opinion drives the price in one direction, then suddenly that opinion reverts. Driven by a swift change in supply and demand, the price turns around and shoots in the opposite direction.

In the next section, we'll talk about additional two-candle patterns that presage trend change. For now, though, answer the questions that follow, then check your answers to gain more insights on the patterns just discussed.

CHECK YOUR UNDERSTANDING

Questions for Chapter Three, Section One: Close Cousins: Piercing, Dark Cloud Covers, Engulfing, and Counterattacks

1. From the choices listed, select three conditions needed for a piercing pattern. _____

    a. Uptrend.

    b. Downtrend.

    c. The first candle is black.

    d. The first candle is white.

    e. The second candle is black.

    f. The second candle is white.

2. From the list in question 1, choose three conditions needed for dark cloud cover. _____

3. As the second session of a piercing pattern pushes more and more deeply into the first candle, it may become a

    a. morning star.

    b. doji star.

    c. dark cloud cover.

    d. bullish engulfing pattern.

4. The opposite pattern to the dark cloud cover is

    a. the bearish engulfing pattern.

    b. the bullish engulfing pattern.

    c. the piercing pattern.

    d. the hammer.

5. A piercing pattern is to a bullish engulfing pattern as a _____ is to a bearish engulfing pattern.

    a. bearish counterattack

    b. bullish counterattack

    c. bearish harami

    d. dark cloud cover

6. For a bullish engulfing pattern, which is true?

    a. The second session's white real body <u>has</u> to wrap around the prior session's shadows.

    b. The second session's white real body <u>has</u> to wrap around the prior session's black real body.

    c. The second session's black real body <u>has</u> to wrap around the prior session's black real body.

    d. The second session's white real body <u>has</u> to wrap around the prior session's white real body.

7. From the following list, choose the two main uses for a bullish engulfing pattern.

    (1) As a bullish continuation signal

    (2) As a bottom reversal signal

    (3) As support

    (4) As resistance

    a. 1 and 2

    b. 2 and 3

    c. 3 and 4

    d. 1 and 4

8. The two candle lines that make up the bullish engulfing pattern have

    a. the same color real bodies.

    b. a black real body followed by a white real body, in a downtrend.

    c. a white real body followed by a black real body, in a downtrend.

    d. two white real bodies in a downtrend.

9. A dark cloud cover is to a piercing pattern as a _____ is to a bullish engulfing pattern.

    a. bearish engulfing pattern

    b. evening star

    c. bearish counterattack

    d. bullish counterattack

10. The most significant difference between the bearish engulfing pattern and a dark cloud cover is

    a. the second session of the bearish engulfing pattern wraps around the prior white real body, while the second session of dark cloud cover closes partially into a prior white real body.

    b. the bearish engulfing pattern wraps around a prior black real body, while the dark cloud cover wraps around the prior black candle.

    c. the dark cloud cover appears after an uptrend, while the bearish engulfing pattern comes after a downtrend.

    d. the dark cloud cover develops after a downtrend, while a bearish engulfing pattern appears after an uptrend.

11. From the following list, which are the requisite conditions for a bearish engulfing pattern?

    (1) The market is in a downtrend.

    (2) On the second session of this pattern, the market should open above the prior session's close.

    (3) On the second session of this pattern, the market should close below the prior session's open.

    (4) On the second session of this pattern, the market must close above the prior session's high.

    a. 1 and 2

    b. 3 and 4

    c. 1 and 3

    d. 2 and 3

12. If an extremely large white candle completes a bullish engulfing pattern, you should

    a. buy immediately on the close of the white candle, since it is so strong.

    b. sell on the close of the white candle, since the market is overbought.

    c. it depends on the risk/reward profile.

    d. None of the above.

13. The important considerations of a bullish counterattack pattern are

    (1) the market is in a downtrend.

    (2) on the second session of the pattern, the market must open under the prior session's high.

(3) on the second session of the pattern, the market must open sharply under the prior session's close, or low.

(4) on the last session of this pattern, the market must close above the prior session's close.

a. 1 and 2

b. 1 and 4

c. 1 and 3

d. 2 and 3

14. One aspect of the bearish counterattack is that today's _____ is the same as yesterday's _____.

a. close, open

b. close, close

c. open, open

d. open, close

15. List the order in which patterns form as a white candle real body moves more deeply into a black candle.

(1) Bullish counterattack

(2) Bullish engulfing pattern

(3) Piercing pattern

(4) Dark cloud cover

a. 1, 2, 3

b. 1, 3, 2

c. 2, 3, 1

d. 4

16. List the order in which patterns form as the close of a black real body moves more deeply into a white candle.

(1) Bearish counterattack.

(2) The patterns are all the same.

(3) Dark cloud cover.

(4) Bearish engulfing pattern.

a. 1, 3, 4

b. 4

c. 1, 2, 3

d. 4, 3, 2

17. Which of the patterns in Exhibit 3.4 are bearish engulfing patterns?

    a. All

    b. 1 and 2

    c. 3 and 4

    d. 1

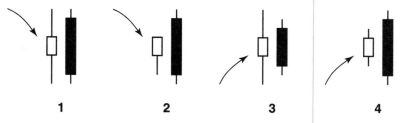

| 1 | 2 | 3 | 4 |

EXHIBIT 3.4   Question 17

Refer to Exhibit 3.5 to answer questions 18 to 20.

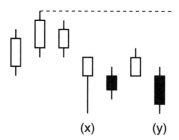

EXHIBIT 3.5   Questions 18–20

18. What candle signal is at x?

    a. Hanging man

    b. Shooting star

    c. Bullish engulfing pattern

    d. None of the above

19. Assume the dashed line is our target on a bounce. Should you buy at the close of candle line x?

    a. Yes, since the candle signal at x is a potentially bullish turning signal.

    b. No, because x has a small real body.

    c. No, because the risk/reward of the trade is not attractive.

    d. Yes, because the risk/reward of the trade is attractive.

20. Assume the dashed line is our target on a bounce. Should you buy at the close of candle line y?

    a. Yes, since the lows of the hammer should be support.

    b. No, because y is a black candle.

    c. No, because the risk/reward of the trade is not attractive.

    d. Yes, because the risk/reward of the trade is attractive.

21. In Exhibit 3.6, after which bullish engulfing pattern is the market most likely to bounce?

    a. 1

    b. 2

    c. 3

    d. 4

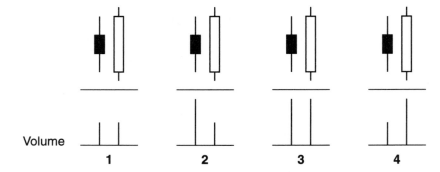

EXHIBIT 3.6   Question 21

Use Exhibit 3.7 to answer questions 22 to 24.

EXHIBIT 3.7   Questions 22–24

22. The pattern shown in Exhibit 3.7 has the same group of candle lines as which pattern?

    a. A bearish engulfing pattern   **c.** A dark cloud cover

    b. A piercing pattern   **d.** A tweezers top

23. Why is the pattern in Exhibit 3.7 not a classic example of this pattern?

    a. The black candle did not open high enough.

    b. The lower shadow of the black candle is not long enough.

    c. The close of the black real body did not intrude deeply enough into the white real body.

    d. The white real body was not long enough.

24. Based on the pattern in Exhibit 3.7, what should you wait for to increase the likelihood of a top reversal?

    a. Wait for doji.

    b. Wait for the next session to close more into the white candle's real body.

    c. Wait for another tall white candle.

    d. Wait for none of the above.

25. In Exhibit 3.8, which is(are) piercing patterns?

    a. 1

    b. 2 and 3

    c. 4

    d. 1 and 3

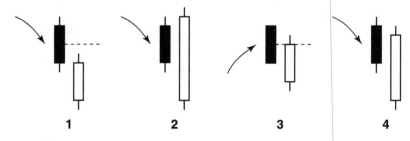

EXHIBIT 3.8   Question 25

26. In Exhibit 3.9, which group(s) of candle signals hint(s) that the bulls are losing momentum?

    a. 1

    b. 2

    c. 2 and 3

    d. 4

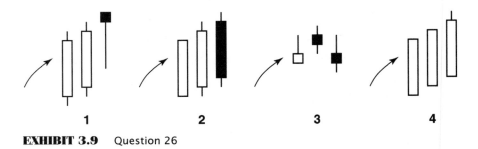

EXHIBIT 3.9   Question 26

27. Which of the bullish counterattack lines shown in Exhibit 3.10 is more likely a reversal?

   a. None of these

   b. All of these

   c. 2

   d. 3

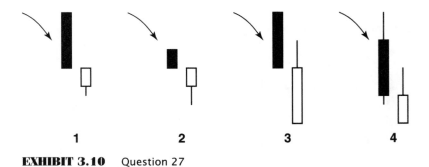

EXHIBIT 3.10   Question 27

Answers for Chapter Three, Section One: Close Cousins: Piercing, Dark Cloud Cover, Engulfing, and Counterattacks

   1. **b, c, f.** The piercing pattern is composed of two candlesticks in a falling market. The first candlestick session in this pattern has a black real body; the second has a long, white real body. The white session opens sharply lower, under the low of the prior black session. Then prices push higher, creating a relatively long, white real body that closes above the midpoint of the prior day's black real body.

2. a, d, e. The dark cloud is the opposite of the piercing pattern. The dark cloud cover is a dual candle pattern that represents a top reversal after an uptrend. The first session of this two-candle pattern is a strong, white real body. The second session's price opens above the prior session's high, meaning above the top of the upper shadow. By the end of the second day's session, however, the market closes deeply within the prior session's white body.

3. d. If the white candle is large enough to close above the opening of the prior black real body, it will become a bullish engulfing pattern.

4. c. The dark cloud cover takes place in an uptrend, forming a black real body closing deeply into a prior white real body. The opposite of that is the piercing pattern. It is a bottom reversal signal that occurs during a market decline, and has a white real body that pushes deeply into the prior black real body.

5. d. This question compares how deeply a real body closes into a prior real body in the two patterns. The piercing pattern has a white candle that closes partially into the prior session's black real body. The bullish engulfing pattern has a white real body that completely wraps around the prior session's black real body. Since a bearish engulfing pattern encompasses all price action of the prior white candle, dark cloud cover, which only partially moves into the prior session's white real body, is the correct answer.

6. b. A bullish engulfing pattern requires that a white real body wraps around the prior black real body during a downtrend. It is not a requisite for a bullish engulfing pattern that the white real body wrap around the prior session's upper or lower shadows.

7. b. Besides acting as a potential bottom reversal signal, the lows of the bullish engulfing pattern can be used as a support level.

8. c. A bullish engulfing pattern consists of a white real body that wraps around a black real body in the context of a downtrend. They have to be consecutive sessions.

9. a. In this analogy, the dark cloud cover is the opposite of the piercing pattern. The opposite of a bullish engulfing pattern is a bearish engulfing pattern.

10. a. The combination of candle lines for both the bearish engulfing pattern and dark cloud cover are the same. Specifically, the market is moving up, and the next session consists of a white candle immediately followed by a candle with a black real body. The main difference between the bearish engulfing pattern and dark cloud cover is that the bearish engulfing pattern's black real body must wrap around the prior session's white real body. The dark cloud cover need only move into the middle of the prior session's white real body.

11. **d.** Since the bearish engulfing pattern consists of a black real body that wraps around a white real body in an uptrend, the open of the second session (i.e., the black real body) must open above the prior session's close.

12. **c.** A bullish engulfing pattern doesn't equate with automatically buying, whether one buys or not on this pattern (or any candle signal) is dependent on the risk/reward profile of the potential trade.

13. **c.** A bullish counterattack pattern occurs during a decline. The first candlestick of this pattern is a long, black real body. The second session opens dramatically lower. At this point, the bears feel confident. The bulls then stage their counterattack by pushing the price back up to the prior close, so the price is virtually unchanged. It's important that the market initially opens deeply under the lows of the preceding session. This gap down shows that the bears have a foothold, at least at the opening bells. But by that session's end, the bulls come back in what the Japanese call a kamikaze battle, to return the market to the prior close.

14. **b.** A bearish counterattack pattern requires that (1) the market is in an uptrend, (2) a white candle is immediately followed by a gap higher opening, and (3) the session that gaps higher closes unchanged, at the same price as the prior white candle session's close.

15. **b.** All these patterns are bottom reversal signals that have a black candle directly followed by a white candle that opened weaker. The difference in these patterns is the extent to which the white candle intrudes into the black candle. The bullish counterattack pattern has as its second candle a white candle that closes at the same price as the prior session's close. A piercing pattern's second session (white) candle closes above the prior session's close. (Ideally, it closes above the center of the prior white candle.) The bullish engulfing pattern develops with a white candle for the second session that completely wraps around the prior session's black real body. The dark cloud cover has a black candle closing in a prior white candle's real body.

16. **a.** The bearish counterattack has as its second candle a black real body that closes at the same price as the prior (white candle) session's close.

The dark cloud cover's first session is a white candle. The second session is a black candle that moves below the prior session's close. (Ideally, the black candle closes at least halfway into the white candle.) The bearish engulfing pattern has as its second session a black real body that completely wraps around the prior session's white real body.

17. **c.** Two criteria for a bearish engulfing pattern are a black real body engulfing a preceding white real body, and the market must be in an uptrend. Although in examples 1 and 2 we see black real bodies wrapping around white real bodies, the trend preceding the pattern was incorrect. Therefore, 3 and 4 meet the requirement for a bearish engulfing pattern.

18. **d.** This is a hammer. The shape of the line is correct and the trend before the line was the requisite downtrend (even though it was a short-term downtrend).

19. **c.** If one buys on the hammer's close, the risk is to the bottom of the lower shadow of the hammer (that should be a support area). Next we have to determine the potential upside of the trade, which in this case is the dashed resistance line. Consequently, we now have our stop-out level (under the low of the hammer's lower shadow) and a price target (the dashed line). Now we ask the pivotal question: Is this a good trade based on the risk/reward profile of this scenario? In this case, with the risk just about the same as the reward, this might be a trade to bypass. This brings out a critical aspect of the candle charts: Even a beautifully defined candlestick line or pattern may not offer an attractive trade because of a poor risk/reward.

20. **d.** While the market is descending at y, we now have a better risk/reward than in the previous question. This is because the hammer is still potential support and we still have the same price target shown by the dashed line. Since at y we are now near the bottom end of the hammer's support area (the bottom of the lower shadow), we have a tighter stop with more upside potential in relation to this stop-out level. Of course, if the market closed under the lows of y, one should consider vacating longs.

21. **d.** In this case, we see volume confirming the potential bullish implications of the bullish engulfing pattern. Specifically, there is light volume on the black real body portion of the bullish engulfing pattern and volume increase on the white turnaround candle. Although choice c also has higher volume on the white candle than the black, answer d has a much higher-volume session on the white candle compared to the black candle than does choice c. This question displays a powerful aspect of the can-

dle charts: All classic Western charting techniques, such as volume in this example, can be easily merged with candle charting techniques.

22. **c.** This is the same combination of candle lines needed for a dark cloud cover. Specifically, the market is in an ascending mode with a black real body that opens above the prior session's high and then closes into the prior session's white real body.

23. **c.** A classic dark cloud cover should have a close higher than the middle of the prior tall white candle, which shows that the bears have intruded deeply into the bulls' territory.

24. **b.** Bearish confirmation of a less-than-ideal dark cloud cover can be obtained by waiting for the next session (after the second session of the dark cloud cover) to see a close that goes more deeply into the white candle that started the dark cloud cover.

25. **c.** A piercing pattern is a potential bottom reversal signal in which the market opens under the prior day's close, or preferably under the prior day's low, and then closes above the middle of the prior black real body. In scenario 1, the close of a white real body did not get deeply enough into the black real body. In scenario 2, the close of a white real body was strong enough that it wrapped around the black real body and so became a bullish engulfing pattern. Scenario 3 did have the same combination of candle lines that is needed for a piercing pattern, but these lines came after an uptrend instead of the necessary downtrend.

26. **c.** In scenario 2, the last two candle lines form a dark cloud cover, which is a potential top reversal signal. In scenario 3, a series of small real bodies typifies a market that is running out of steam. In scenario 1, although the last candle is a hanging man line, we would need bearish confirmation of that line to turn negative. Scenario 4 shows a series of relatively tall white candles with higher highs, lows, and closes and therefore no signs of losing bullish momentum.

27. **d.** The theory of the bullish counterattack is that the market should open robustly lower than the prior session and close unchanged from that prior session. Such a close on the second session proves that although the market opened sharply lower, the bears could not sustain control of the market into the close. In Exhibit 3.10, the only scenario that had a sharply lower opening was 3.

SECTION TWO

The Harami and Harami Cross, Morning and Evening Stars

In this section, we're going to discuss more candle patterns that are formed by a combination of single candle lines. First, we'll look at an interesting two-candle pattern called the harami, and a variation on that pattern known as a harami cross. Then we'll delve into a powerful three-candle pattern—the star pattern—renowned for calling bottom and top reversals. The star pattern incorporates spinning tops and doji. As you remember, we discussed the shooting star before. Now we'll explore morning stars, evening stars, and stars that include a doji, called morning doji stars and evening doji stars.

In this section you will learn . . .

- The importance of the harami and harami cross
- The differences between the harami and harami cross
- The power underpinning the harami cross
- How to differentiate between the harami and the engulfing pattern
- How the harami pattern compares to the Western inside day
- The criteria for morning and evening stars
- How morning and evening stars call bottom and top reversals
- How volume activity intensifies star signals

Key terms to watch for:

- Harami
- Harami cross
- Petrifying pattern
- Inside day
- Star
- Morning star
- Evening star

GETTING STARTED

In previous sections, we talked about single candle lines called spinning tops. These small real lines are components in the reversal pattern referred to as the *harami*.

As shown in Exhibit 3.11, the first real body of this pattern is an unusually long black or white real body. The next candle consists of a small real body, which is completely within the prior real body.

The color of the real bodies in this pattern is unimportant: They can be opposite or the same.

As you can see, like all candle patterns we've discussed so far, the harami is a reversal pattern. The Japanese say that when the harami pattern (Exhibit 3.11A) appears, a preceding rally or downtrend is losing its breath. The bearish harami tells us that despite the bullish white real body that moved the market higher, the tiny real body that follows indicates uncertainty and indecision. As you learned in previous sections, the limited price range of the small real body—especially when it follows a real body with a wide price range—shows that trend velocity has weakened.

On the other hand, when a bullish harami (Exhibit 3.11B) appears in a decline or downtrend, the selling pressure demonstrated by the first long, real

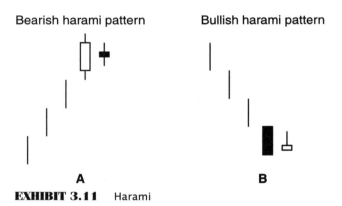

Bearish harami pattern   Bullish harami pattern

A   B

EXHIBIT 3.11   Harami

SIDE LIGHT

The term *harami* is derived from a Japanese word that means pregnant. The first candle has a large body (the mother) with the small real body (the baby) inside it.

If both the first and second candles of a harami pattern are white, it is called a white-white harami. If the first is black and the second is white, it is called a black-white harami. I just call them both harami since the colors of the real bodies are not significant in this pattern.

---

body in the pattern is apparent. Then the second tiny real body forms. The bears suddenly lose momentum; they are unable to close the market at or below the prior candle's close. Uncertainty sets in, as the harami foretells a possible reversal and trend break. Do you understand how this pattern tells you an important story about market environment, with its accompanying change of sentiment? If the second real body is a doji instead of a spinning top, it is called a *harami cross* (Exhibit 3.12).

Next, we'll discuss an intriguing pattern known as the star. Indeed, this pattern is a star when it comes to calling top and bottom reversals!

A *star* is a small real body (think spinning top) that gaps away from the long real body preceding it in an uptrend or downtrend. The third candle in the formation also should gap away from the real body of the star, leaving the star's real body isolated at the top or bottom of an uptrend or downtrend. Ideally, the real bodies should not overlap, although the star's real body can intrude into the prior candle's shadow.

The star's real body represents a tug-of-war between the bulls and bears. It's a similar concept to that of the harami—a strong move in an uptrend or downtrend, directly followed by an indecisive time period. The star represents a stronger initial surge in the prevailing trend, however, before opposite forces arrive to quell it.

Bearish harami cross   Bullish harami cross

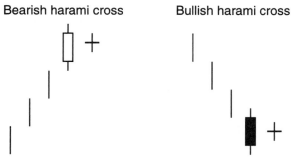

EXHIBIT 3.12   Harami Crosses

The star is the middle portion of two candle patterns called the morning star and evening star (Exhibit 3.13). The *morning star* is a bottom reversal pattern that derives its picturesque name from Mercury, the morning star that appears just before sunrise. Just as the morning star precedes daylight, the morning star candle pattern potentially presages higher prices.

Three candle lines form this pattern. First, in the context of a downtrend, a long, black candle develops, assuring the bears that they continue to be in command. Then a small real body or spinning top appears, gapping down at the open of its session and delighting the confident bears. The star (the middle portion of the morning star) completes its formation in a tight price range, without rising back to close into the prior black real body, although it may rise to an intraday high that infringes on the black candle's lower shadow. The final candle of the morning star pattern is a white real body that moves deeply into the first session's black candle. This panics the bears, as the white candle proves that the bulls have taken control and reversed the downtrend.

The morning star's bearish counterpart is the *evening star*. Three candle lines make up this top reversal signal. In the context of an uptrend, a long

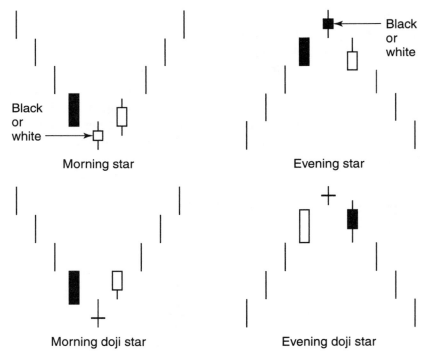

EXHIBIT 3.13   Morning and Evening Stars

white candle appears, convincing the bulls that the rally will continue. Then the star appears in the form of a small real body that classically gaps up from the white candle's closing price. The star's real body (black or white) remains isolated as the next candle confirms the trend top by gapping away from the star and producing a long, black real body that pushes into the white candle's real body. The final candle seals the fate of the bulls as the bears grab control and push the market downward.

If the middle portion of either the morning or evening star is a doji instead of a spinning top, the pattern is called a *morning doji star* or *evening doji star* (Exhibit 3.13).

The valuable harami, harami cross, and star patterns offer you more reversal patterns to place in your trader's toolbox. Your ability to recognize these patterns on charts of any time frame will add to your trend forecasting and money-management skills.

In the next two sections of this chapter, we'll discuss more candle patterns that signal top and bottom reversals. We'll also explore an entirely different concept, that of candles in continuation patterns. First, though, please complete the questions that follow. Be sure to check the answers that follow the questions for added information.

CHECK YOUR UNDERSTANDING

Questions for Chapter Three, Section Two: The Harami and Harami Cross, Morning and Evening Stars

1. The harami is a _____ signal.

    a. bullish reversal   **c.** continuation

    b. bearish reversal   **d.** bullish or bearish reversal

2. The harami pattern is

   a. a small real body followed by a long real body.

   b. a small real body that must form inside the prior long real body.

   c. two consecutive small real bodies

   d. Both b and c

3. Which statement is true about the color of the real bodies for a harami?

   a. Both sessions *must* have the same-color real bodies.

   b. Both sessions *can* have the same-color real bodies.

   c. The first session must be black, and the second session must be white.

   d. Both sessions must have opposite-color real bodies.

4. An engulfing pattern consists of a long real body wrapping around a small real body. Which candlestick pattern has the reverse scenario—that is, a long real body followed by a small real body?

   a. A piercing pattern

   b. A dark cloud cover

   c. A harami pattern

   d. Both a and b

5. What is the difference between the harami and the harami cross?

   a. They are the same.

   b. The harami cross has same-color real bodies.

   c. The harami cross forms with a doji as the second candle instead of a small real body.

   d. The harami cross must come after an uptrend.

6. What is the difference between a Western inside day and a harami pattern?

   a. They are the same.

   b. A harami requires that the open-close range be within the prior session's open-close range, whereas an inside day requires a high-low range within the prior session's high-low range.

   c. A harami requires a low that is below the prior session's low, but an inside day requires the low to be above the prior session's low.

   d. None of the above

7. From the list that follows, choose four conditions needed for a morning star. _____

   1. Uptrend.

   2. Downtrend.

   3. The first candle of the pattern is black.

   4. The first candle of the pattern is white.

   5. The second candle of the pattern is white.

   6. The second candle of the pattern is either black or white.

   7. The third candle of the pattern is white.

   8. The third candle of the pattern is black.

8. From the list in question 7, choose four conditions required for an evening star. _____

9. A morning star pattern is a potential

   a. top reversal signal.

   b. bearish continuation signal.

   c. bullish continuation signal.

   d. bottom reversal signal.

10. When an evening or morning star pattern develops, the second real body of that pattern <u>must</u> be

   a. black.

   b. white.

   c. small.

   d. large.

11. Which part of the evening or morning star pattern represents the star portion?

   a. The first candle line

   b. The second candle line

   c. The third candle line

   d. The fourth candle line

12. Which session of the evening star pattern represents the reversal?

   a. The first session

   b. The second session

   c. The fourth session

   d. None of the above

13. If the star portion of the evening star is a doji, that pattern becomes
    a. an evening doji star.
    b. a tweezers top.
    c. a harami cross.
    d. a tri-star.

14. In Exhibit 3.14, which is(are) evening star(s)?
    a. 3
    b. 4
    c. 1
    d. Both 3 and 4

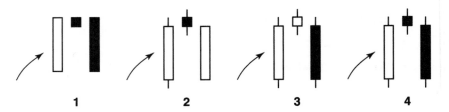

EXHIBIT 3.14   Question 14

15. In Exhibit 3.15, which is(are) harami patterns?
    a. All
    b. None
    c. Both 2 and 3
    d. 2

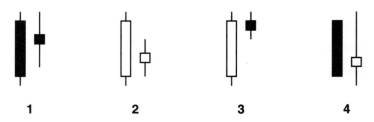

EXHIBIT 3.15   Question 15

Answers for Chapter Three, Section Two: The Harami and Harami Cross, Morning and Evening Stars

1. **d.** The harami can be either a potential top reversal or a bottom reversal signal. In the context of an uptrend, the pattern appears as an unusually long, white real body immediately followed by a small real body (black or white). This represents a potentially bearish harami. On the flipside, in a descending market, a long black real body forms first, followed by a small real body (black or white), again encompassed by the larger real body's price range. This represents a bullish harami.

2. **b.** A harami pattern can take place during an uptrend or downtrend. In an uptrend, a long white real body is followed by a spinning top that forms within the prior candle's real body. In a downtrend, a long, black real body is followed immediately by a spinning top that forms within the longer candle's real body.

3. **b.** The second real body of the harami pattern can be white or black. For example, if a white real body is the first portion of the harami, and a small, white real body is the next session, the Japanese refer to this as a white-white harami.

4. **c.** The harami is the reverse of an engulfing pattern. Whereas an engulfing pattern presents a long candle engulfing the previous real body, the harami emerges as an unusually long real body followed by a very small real body. After a downtrend, the appearance of a harami shows, as it is expressed in Japan, that the decline is exhausting itself. A harami topping an advance shows that the market has a poor chance of rising.

5. **c.** The harami cross is sometimes called the petrifying pattern. Because it forms with a doji as the second candle, this pattern often portrays more likelihood of a reversal than the traditional harami.

6. **b.** Although the inside day and the harami appear similar, the harami has a major advantage in that it may give a signal not available with the Western inside session. Specifically, the inside session requires that the current session's high-low range is within the prior session's high-low range. However, the harami requires only that the current session's real body be within the prior session's real body, even if the current session's high is above the prior session's high or the current session's low falls below the prior session's low. This means that the harami may provide a reversal signal that is not apparent with the Western inside day.

7. **2, 3, 6, 7.** The morning star is a three-candlestick bottom reversal pattern. It is made up of a tall, black real body followed by a small real body.

The small real body gaps lower than the prior real body. The third session is a white real body that moves well within the first candle's black real body.

8. **1, 4, 6, 8.** The evening star is a three-candlestick pattern. The criteria for this pattern include a market in an uptrend. Then a long, white candle appears, followed by a small real body. The small real body can be either black or white and ideally should not touch the real body of the first candle. The third candle of this pattern is a black real body that ideally does not touch the second real body. The third candle closes well into the white candle line that made up the first candle of this pattern.

9. **d.** In the context of a downtrend, the morning star is a three-candlestick reversal signal. The first candle, a long, black real body, shows that the bears are still in control. The second candle is a small real body that shows the bears are losing momentum. This small real body should not touch the prior black candle. The final turning signal and completion of the morning star pattern arrives with the third candle, which should be a tall, white candle that moves well into the first candle's real body.

10. **c.** In both the evening and the morning star, the middle candle line must be a spinning top or doji. The color of the spinning top is not relevant.

11. **b.** In both the evening and morning star pattern, the second session, or spinning top, is referred to as the star.

12. **d.** The third black candle, which moves well into the first candle's white real body, completes the session.

13. **a.** If a doji appears as the second candle line (instead of a spinning top) in a morning or evening star pattern, it is renamed a morning doji star or evening doji star.

14. **d.** Scenarios 3 and 4 are evening stars. The color of the middle portion (the small real body) of an evening star can be black or white. Scenario 1 is not a classic evening star because in an ideal evening star the second real body should not be touching the first real body. In scenario 2, although the grouping of candle lines is correct for an evening star, the last candle should be black, not white.

15. **a.** These are all examples of harami patterns. The definition of a harami pattern is a small real body within a prior unusually long real body. The color of the real body does not matter. Even if the shadows of the second session of the harami are outside the real body of the first session, it is still a harami if the real body of the second session is within the real body of the first session.

SECTION THREE

Picturesque Storytellers: Tweezers, Crows, and Soldiers

In this section, we'll continue to explore interesting candle patterns that tell us more about the mood and manner of market environment. Although the recent price action of a chart is important, earlier price history can also contribute to our assessment of future price movement. The stories candle patterns tell us, present and past, all add to our ability to evaluate potential opportunities that will contribute to our success as traders and investors.

Now, on to the candle patterns known as tweezers, crows, and soldiers. The knowledge you've acquired in previous sections will make the following patterns easy to understand.

In this section you will learn . . .

- The construction of the candle pattern the Japanese call tweezers
- How tweezers signal trend changes on long-term charts
- How tweezers incorporate other candle patterns
- The definition of *three black crows* and the signal they give
- The pattern known as three advancing soldiers and variations on the pattern
- Caveats pertaining to three advancing soldiers

Key terms to watch for:

- Tweezers
- Tweezers top
- Tweezers bottom
- Three black crows
- Three advancing soldiers

GETTING STARTED

The candle pattern known as *tweezers* consists of two or more candle lines with matching highs or lows. The name is derived from the appearance of their formation. The *tweezers top* occurs in a rising market when two or more consecutive highs match each other, thus giving the image of the two prongs of a tweezers (Exhibit 3.16). (Since tweezers pinch, the connotation is that the trend is getting pinched.) A *tweezers bottom* takes place in a declining market, when two successive lows are equal.

Ideally, the tweezers pattern should develop with the first session incorporating a long real body. In a declining market, this would probably be a long black candlestick; in a rising market, it would finalize as a long white candlestick.

The second session is interesting because it has many variations. It's best—but not absolutely necessary—when this session forms with a small real body. You are already familiar with the candle lines that may provide this component. For example, a tweezers top might finish with a hanging man, a

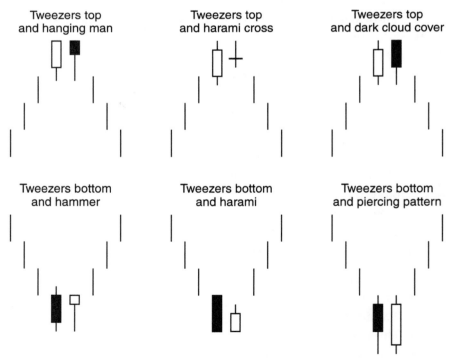

EXHIBIT 3.16   Tweezers Tops and Tweezers Bottoms

shooting star, or a dark cloud cover pattern. A tweezers bottom could culminate with a hammer, harami cross, or piercing pattern.

With the first long real body and the second smaller real body integrating two consecutive highs, the tweezers top tells us that the bullish force of the long white candle began to dissipate with the small real body of the second candle line. Also, since the second candle cannot make a higher high than the first candle, the tweezers top adds to the outlook of a slakening of demand.

The tweezers bottom begins with a long black real body carrying the happy bears to victory. But the next candle, with the same lows and often completed with a small real body, switches victory to uncertainty. As buying bulls start nibbling, the bear's failure to press the second session to a lower low intensifies their angst. Naturally, the next candle will help confirm the potential reversal.

We assign little importance to two consecutive highs or lows shown on a daily or intraday chart unless other defining signals are present. In and of themselves, they are not noteworthy.

If you are a long-term trader or investor, you probably study weekly and monthly charts to obtain a longer perspective. So, as opposed to shorter time frames of intraday and daily charts, tweezers tops and bottoms that appear on weekly and monthly charts potentially indicate important reversal signals. For example, if a declining stock finished the current week by successfully holding last week's low, it could be the start of a base for a future rally. Conversely, if a 15-minute candle on an intraday chart successfully holds at the prior candle's low, it is not as significant.

The next candle pattern appears only at high price levels, or in the context of a mature uptrend. The Japanese gave it the quaint name, three black crows. Also called three winged crows, the *three black crows* pattern consists of three black candles that should close at or near their lows (Exhibit 3.17).

Three black crows

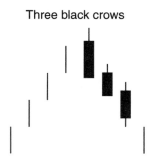

EXHIBIT 3.17 Three Black Crows

SIDE LIGHT

The Japanese refer to the opposite of the three black crows pattern as three advancing white soldiers, or three white soldiers. Again, as with other candle patterns, there is a military connection.

The first candle appears near the top of an uptrend that's already starting to roll over, or move down. Each session's open should ideally take place within the previous session's real body.

The three black crows pattern sends useful signals for long-term traders and investors. By the time the pattern concludes with the completion of the third black candle, it's already obvious that the market has fallen significantly from its recent high. Were you holding a prospective long-term position and a three black crows pattern appeared on a weekly chart, in conjunction with other indicators, it might warn you to take partial or all profits.

As we can see in Exhibit 3.18, *three white soldiers* appear as three long white candles exhibiting consecutively higher prices. This is a continuation pattern, and optimally, each candle should close at or near its high. The lines form an orderly, ongoing rise, with each candle opening within or close to the prior candle's real body. For this pattern, trend is not critical. The soldiers may begin an upward climb out of a downtrend reversal or may emerge during a rally. In these instances, the pattern suggests positive momentum ahead.

Pundits are fond of saying, "Trading is war." The patterns in this section—tweezers tops and bottoms, three black crows, and three white soldiers—provide you with extra ammunition to carry into battle. In the market combat zone, the more knowledge you have, the more likely you are to succeed. That's true now, more than ever, with volatility occurring as an everyday event.

Three white soldiers

EXHIBIT 3.18   Three White Soldiers

KEY POINT

A caveat regarding the three white soldiers pattern: Although the candles display a healthy rise in the market, they do not necessarily give you a buy signal. When the candles move to an extended price range, be careful of entering long positions. Overbought markets usually consolidate or retrace after prolonged price rises. The proper long entry may appear after a pullback to price support.

In the next section, we will discuss the powerful candlestick continuation pattern known as windows. The window represents the Japanese version of the Western gap, and it provides us with a host of compelling signals.

Before you go on to that section, though, answer the questions that follow. Take your time to assess how much knowledge you absorbed from the material discussed in this section. That's the best way to obtain the most from this course book.

CHECK YOUR UNDERSTANDING

Questions for Chapter Three, Section Three: Tweezers, Crows, and Soldiers

1. One condition that a tweezers top must display is

    a. matching highs.

    b. matching real bodies.

    c. matching mid-points.

    d. matching lows.

2. Ideally, in a mature advance, a tweezers top consists of

    a. a long black candle followed by a doji.

    b. a long white candle followed by an evening star doji.

    c. a long white candle followed by a smaller real body that has the same high.

    d. a long black candle followed by an island reversal.

3. A tweezers bottom that forms at the potential culmination of a decline could form as

   a. a small-bodied black candle followed by a bearish belt-hold.

   b. a morning doji star.

   c. a harami pattern with equal lows on both candle lines.

   d. a piercing pattern followed by a harami.

4. On a weekly chart, a tweezers top shows that

   a. this week's high is the same as last week's high.

   b. the top of the real bodies have the same lows.

   c. the top of the real bodies have the same highs.

   d. None of the above.

5. One condition for a three black crows pattern is

   a. three black candles.

   b. three black spinning tops.

   c. three bullish belt-holds.

   d. three dark cloud covers in a row.

6. Three black crows signify a bearish market environment when they appear in

   a. a box range.

   b. an uptrend.

   c. a downtrend.

   d. directly after a bullish piercing pattern.

7. The signal generated by three black crows is best utilized by

   a. day traders.

   b. market makers.

   c. New York Stock Exchange specialists.

   d. long-term traders and investors.

8. A condition for the three white soldiers pattern is

   a. they appear in a sharp downtrend.

   b. they emerge in a box range.

   c. they develop in an uptrend.

   d. None of the above.

9. Ideally, the real bodies that make up the three white soldiers pattern should move in

    a. an orderly rise with consecutively higher closes.

    b. a sideways pattern.

    c. an uptrend that includes a 50% retracement.

    d. an uptrend that includes a doji.

10. Why could you call three white soldiers the "good news, bad news" pattern?

    a. Because the candles look strong, but they are really weak.

    b. Although the candles are moving up, short selling is responsible for the uptrend.

    c. The candle's rise is only a rebound in a bear market.

    d. Because a market that rises for three consecutive days may be in danger of becoming overbought.

11. Match the patterns shown in Exhibit 3.19 with their candlestick term.

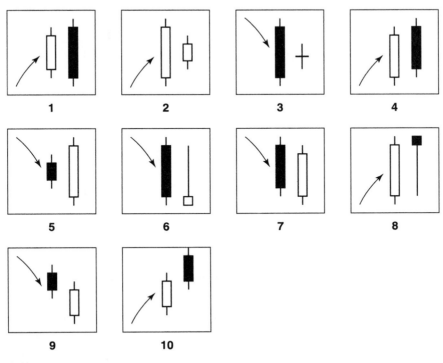

EXHIBIT 3.19   Question 11

Candlestick Name	Figure Number
a. Bearish engulfing pattern	_____
b. Bullish engulfing pattern	_____
c. Harami	_____
d. Harami cross	_____
e. Tweezers top	_____
f. Tweezers bottom	_____
g. Dark cloud cover	_____
h. Piercing pattern	_____
i. Bullish counterattack	_____
j. Bearish counterattack	_____

12. In Exhibit 3.20, which of these is(are) advancing three soldiers?

   a. 1

   b. 2

   c. 3

   d. Both 2 and 4

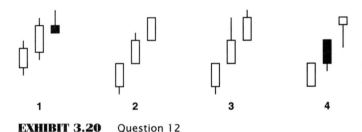

EXHIBIT 3.20   Question 12

Answers for Chapter Three, Section Three: Tweezers, Crows, and Soldiers

1. **a.** The criterion for a tweezers top is that it must be formed of two consecutive candle lines that share equal highs.

2. **c.** The ideal tweezers top consists of a long white candle followed by a smaller real body that has the same high.

3. **c.** A tweezers bottom that forms at the potential culmination of a decline could form as a harami pattern with equal lows on both candle lines. The first candle in a bullish harami is a long white real body that appears in a decline. The second is a smaller real body that resides within the opening

and closing price range of the first candle. As long as both candles have the same low—whether formed by shadows or real bodies—the pattern can be designated a tweezers bottom.

4. **a.** On a weekly chart showing a tweezers top, this week's high would be the same as last week's high. The tweezers may be composed of real bodies, shadows, and/or doji. Tweezers occurs on consecutive sessions, yet are not a vital reversal signal on an intraday or daily chart. They take on extra importance when they contain other bearish (for a top reversal), or bullish (for a bottom reversal) candlestick signals. For those who utilize longer time perspectives, tweezers tops and bottoms on weekly and monthly candlestick charts may represent significant reversal patterns. A low made last week, or month, that successfully tested, could be a base for a rally. A low made yesterday, that is successfully tested today, however, is less likely to hold as a base, as the time frame is shorter.

5. **a.** The three black crows pattern consists of three falling candles, all with black real bodies.

6. **b.** Three black crows appear as a top reversal. Consequently, this pattern must come during an uptrend.

7. **d.** With all candle patterns, the signal is only valid when the final candle is complete. With this pattern it means the third black candle. As such, it may be best used by longer-term traders and investors. This ominous signal gives a hint of trouble with the first black crow, which may form as a dark cloud cover, or other top reversal candle line. By the time the third black crow develops completely, it is apparent that the bears are in control. But by then the market may have moved well off its highs; therefore, if you sell on this pattern, you should have a longer-term perspective.

8. **d.** The trend is not important with the three soliders. The major condition for the three white soldiers pattern is that there are three white candles each with a higher close and that each session closes at or near its highs.

9. **a.** The real bodies that make up the three white soldiers pattern should move in an uptrend, and each white candle should close with a higher price than the previous candle.

10. **d.** The good news: Three strong white candles forecast a market moving in healthy rise. Not-so-good news: By the completion of the third candle, the market may be overextended or nearing a resistance area. In those cases, it's best to wait for a buying setup after the market consolidates, or retraces. When it bounces off support and shows signs of resuming the uptrend, a buying setup may emerge.

11. **a.** 1

   b. 5

   c. 2

   d. 3

   e. 8

   f. 6

   g. 4

   h. 7

   i. 9

   j. 10

12. **b.** Three white or three advancing soldiers is a group of three white candlesticks with consecutively higher closes, with each of the closes near the highs of the session. These three white candlesticks presage more strength if they appear after a period of stable prices or at a low price area.

SECTION FOUR

Disjointed Candles: Rising and Falling Windows

In previous sections, we've studied reversal patterns. These patterns have suggested we take action, whether to open a new position or apply money-management rules to close a position. Now we are going to explore a Japanese continuation pattern that implies the prior trend will continue. This pattern, called a window, is synonymous with the Western pattern known as a gap. We'll discuss the fundamental concepts of windows and how they apply in different patterns. We'll also talk about some general concepts as they apply to trends.

In this section you will learn . . .

- The definition of window
- How a rising window differs from a falling window
- How windows act as support and resistance areas
- Why closing prices are so important when closing windows
- Why size doesn't matter with windows
- Where key support areas are located in large windows
- Why it's important to trade with the trend

Key terms to watch for:

- Window
- Rising window
- Falling window
- Price vacuum

101

GETTING STARTED

In technical analysis, we generally talk about two kinds of patterns: reversal patterns and continuation patterns. By now you are familiar with the action that takes place in a reversal pattern, meaning a change in direction. If you are a trader, you spend the majority of your time assessing charts and looking for potential trend reversals; that is where you typically enter and exit positions. Continuation patterns suggest that the trend before the pattern will continue, whether up or down.

A window is the same as a Western gap, but the Japanese have unique uses for windows (details follow in this section). A *window* means there is a price zone in which no trades take place, or a price vacuum. For example, stock XYZ has a high at $50. If the low of the next session is $52, there is a $2 *rising window*. If, however, stock XYZ has a low at $50, with the next session's high at $48, we would say it has gapped down $2 and therefore a $2 *falling window* exists.

A *rising window* is a bullish signal. The price vacuum between the prior candle's high and the current session's low means the bulls are in control and willing to pay up. A falling window is a bearish signal. The absence of price activity between the prior candle's low and the current session's high shows the bears are driving the market down, with no competition from the bulls.

The Japanese advise, "Go in the direction of the window." This makes sense, as windows are continuation signals. If the bulls are willing to skip several price levels and pay higher prices for a security, then they are indeed in control. Conversely, if prices are so weak that bears can force them to plunge below a certain range, then the selling pressure is not to be doubted.

 SIDE LIGHT

For a quick demonstration of how gaps can be filled on an intraday basis, watch a stock that gaps up a point or more at the open. Since some market professionals make a living from *fading the gap*, or trading in the opposite direction from the gap move: If a stock gaps higher a substantial amount at the open, the pro will sell it short for a quick trade. If enough selling pressure occurs, the stock will drop enough to fill a portion, or all, of the price vacuum. (Please don't try this technique yourself, unless you are a *very* experienced trader. It involves extremely high risk.)

One of the most common misunderstandings about rising and falling windows is identifying the part of the candle session that constitutes a price limit. Some think that if real bodies do not touch, the space between is a window. This is incorrect. With rising and falling windows, there must be a space—whether narrow or wide—where candle highs and lows do not intersect. If shadows intersect, there is no window. There must be a *price vacuum*, or space between price levels, for a window to be valid.

One of the most useful signals offered to us by rising and falling windows is summed up by another Japanese saying: "Corrections stop at the window." That means windows often become support and resistance areas. You can see how this works in Exhibit 3.21, with windows acting as springboards of support and resistance.

When a rising window occurs, the *entire space* of that window is considered a support area. Therefore, if you have a long position that just developed a rising window, you can expect that window to act as support if the market pulls back. If the price retraces to the bottom of the window, but *does not close below it*, then support has not been broken. If, however, the market closes below the window's bottom, then support *has* been broken. Consequently, the most important area of a rising window is the bottom of that window.

The same is true for a falling window. When a falling window forms, the entire price vacuum establishes a resistance area. If you are considering a

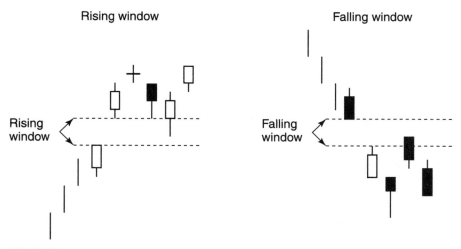

EXHIBIT 3.21   Rising and Falling Windows

short sale, you can regard the window as price resistance when (if) the security rallies. If the price rallies to the top of the window, but *does not close above it,* that resistance stays intact. However, if the price rallies through the falling window and *closes* above it, the resistance area is broken; no short sale should be entered. Thus, the top of a falling window is its critical resistance area.

In the next unit, you will find many different examples of rising and falling windows to study. Just as a picture is worth a thousand words, these diagrams and real-world charts will help you understand more thoroughly how windows act as strong components of price patterns.

CHECK YOUR UNDERSTANDING

Questions for Chapter Three, Section Four: Disjointed Candles: Rising and Falling Windows

1. A rising window on a daily chart takes place when

   a. two consecutive real bodies do not touch.

   b. today's lower shadow is the same as yesterday's lower shadow.

   c. today's lower shadow is exactly the same as yesterday's upper shadow.

   d. None of the above.

2. A falling window is a

   a. bullish continuation signal.

   b. bearish continuation signal.

   c. bullish reversal signal.

   d. bearish reversal signal.

3. The minimum distance for a valid window is

   a. 50 cents.

   b. 1 dollar.

   c. any amount—even 1 cent.

   d. 10 cents.

4. The larger the rising window, the

   a. more significant the subsequent move should be.

   b. larger the support zone.

    c. smaller the support zone.

    d. more likely the market will reverse from up to down.

5. Which part of the rising window should be support?

    a. The top of the window only

    b. The bottom of the window only

    c. The entire window

    d. The 50% retracement level within the window only

6. In a major downtrend, a bullish candle signal could be used to

    a. go short.

    b. go long.

    c. step aside.

    d. wait for the bounce to consider selling.

7. When a bearish candle signal emerges in an uptrending market, the more overbought the market, the _____ vulnerable it is.

    a. less

    b. more

    c. equally

    d. One has no bearing on the other.

8. The more candlestick or Western indicators that merge together at the same support or resistance area,

    a. the more significant the move away from support or resistance.

    b. the more likely a reversal.

    c. the less likely a reversal.

    d. None of the above.

9. In Exhibit 3.22, which of the choices below is(are) windows?

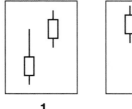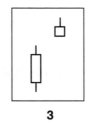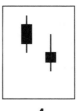

1   **2**   **3**   **4**

EXHIBIT 3.22   Question 9

a. Both 2 and 3

b. All

c. Both 1 and 4

d. 2

Use Exhibit 3.23 to answer questions 10 to 13.

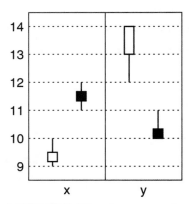

EXHIBIT 3.23   Questions 10 to 13

10. Define support shown by the rising window at X.

    a. Zone from 10 to 9

    b. Zone from 11 to 10

    c. Zone from 12 to 11

    d. 11

11. What is the most important support area of this rising window at X?

    a. 12

    b. 11

    c. 10

    d. 9

12. Define resistance as shown by the falling window at Y.

    a. 12 to 13

    b. 10 to 11

    c. 11 to 12

    d. 10 to 12

13. What is the most important resistance area of this falling window?

    a. 12

    b. 14

    c. 11

    d. 12

Answer the next two questions based on Exhibit 3.24.

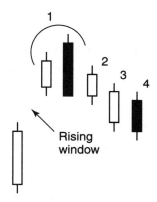

EXHIBIT 3.24   Questions 14 and 15

14. What pattern is shown at 1?

    a. Dark cloud cover

    b. Tower top

    c. Bullish engulfing pattern

    d. Bearish engulfing pattern

15. What is bearish confirmation of this pattern? (Hint: There is a small rising window.)

    a. Candle line 3

    b. Candle line 4

    c. Candle line 2

    d. On the black session that completes the bearish engulfing pattern

Answers for Chapter Three, Section Four: Disjointed Candles: Rising and Falling Windows

1. **d.** A rising window takes place on a daily chart when today's low is above yesterday's high. In other words, today's lower shadow should reside above yesterday's upper shadow, with no price overlap.

2. **b.** A falling window is a bearish continuation signal and should act as resistance on rallies. A bearish continuation signal means that the downtrend in force before the signal remains intact after the signal. A rising window is a bullish continuation signal, which means the rally preceding the rising window remains in effect after the rising window emerges. Therefore, corrections that fall to that rising window should use it for potential support.

3. **c.** With a window, size does not matter. Even if the window is only 1 cent wide, it is still valid. The window should act as support or resistance, depending on whether it's a rising or falling window.

4. **b.** A large rising window means there is a big zone of support. Remember, the entire window represents potential support, and we don't know beforehand how far—or if—the market will pull into the window before bouncing. Choice (a) is not correct, since candle charting techniques do not project moves. Therefore, even if a market has a large rising window, it does not necessarily mean the rally will be substantially more powerful.

5. **c.** In both rising and falling windows, the entire window is important. It becomes potential support for a rising window, and resistance for a falling window.

6. **d.** No matter what technical tools you are using, you should consider always trading in the direction of the major trend. If the major (long-term) trend is down, and a bullish candlestick signal appears, you would be more prudent to use a potential bounce from this signal to sell on a rally. Although the candlestick pattern described in the question was bullish, selling rallies is in line with the bearish nature of the prevailing trend. This also means that if a major bull trend is in force and we see a bullish candlestick signal in a down move, we could consider initiating a long position. That action would keep us trading in the direction of the major trend.

7. **b.** One of the most important criteria for using candle charts is to remember that these patterns mainly offer reversal signals. If the market is overextended, either to the upside or the downside, the odds of a rever-

sal with a candlestick signal are greatly enhanced. Therefore, if a bearish candle signal emerges and the market is greatly overbought, the market is more likely to reverse.

8. **b.** Although we are focusing mainly on candle charts in this book, it should be remembered that the power of candles is enhanced by combining them with Western charting techniques. Specifically, if there is a strong Western technical signal, such as a moving average that has worked well as support, and a candle signal appears at that moving average's support level, the chances of a turnaround increase. Remember, though, that even if a combination of candlestick signals and Western indicators converge at the same support or resistance area and greatly increase the likelihood of a reversal, the indicators do not project the extent of the move.

9. **a.** Windows are synonymous with gaps in Western technicals. This means that there should be no price overlap between one session and the prior session. Examples 2 and 3 display falling and rising windows, respectively. In examples 1 and 4, although the real bodies are not touching, these are not windows since the shadows overlap. With windows, no part of the candle line, including the shadows, can overlap.

10. **b.** The zone of support for the rising window is the whole window. In this exhibit the window runs from 11 to 10 and as such becomes a potential support zone.

11. **c.** While the whole zone is potential support (from 11 to 10), the pivotal support of rising windows is at the bottom of the window. In this example, the bottom of the window is at 10.

12. **c.** The falling window's zone of resistance is the entire window. In this exhibit, since the market gapped down from 12 to 11, that becomes the resistance area.

13. **a.** Even though for a falling window the entire window is resistance, the most important resistance is at the top of the window. In this case, the top of the falling window is at 12.

14. **d.** The black real body wrapping around the white real body in an uptrend forms a bearish engulfing pattern.

15. **b.** Although a bearish engulfing pattern is typically a top reversal signal, it is critical to place the candles in the context of recent market activity. In this example, the white candle of the bearish engulfing pattern gapped higher than the prior session and in doing so formed a bullish rising

window. Therefore, we have a bearish engulfing pattern that formed at the potential support of a bullish rising window. Based on the theory that a rising window should be support, one would have to wait for a close under this rising window to confirm the bearish implications of the bearish engulfing pattern. The close under this rising window came on session 4. Observe how at session 3 the market did break under the rising window's support on an intraday basis, not a closing basis. To confirm a break of the window's support one would need a close under the bottom of that rising window. This occurred on session 4.

CHAPTER FOUR

Taking Advantage of Market Opportunities

A s the Japanese proverb states, "Make use of your opportunities." In this chapter I show some practical applications of how candle charts will let you take advantage of market opportunities. The examples in Section 1 of this chapter provide illustrations of the following real-world applications.

- Using candle charts to preserve capital
- How candle charts give early reversal signals
- How candle charts can confirm support or resistance areas
- Using a confluence of candle signals to confirm support or resistance
- The ease of combining Western technical tools with candle charts
- Obtaining a price target
- Harnessing the insights of the candles to enter and exit a trade
- Using intraday trading signals
- The technique of using a longer time frame chart to get support or resistance and a short time frame to issue the buy or sell signal

Section 2 of this chapter applies the trading precepts given in Chapters One, Two, and Three. Keep in mind that the techniques shown in the rest of this chapter can be applied to any market you are trading—futures, equities, fixed-income—and any time frame—from a 1-minute to a monthly chart. In addition, option traders can also use candle signals as a timing mechanism. The exception to this universality of use for candles is that the market has to have an open, high, low, and close. Tick charts and daily mutual funds, for example, can't have candle charts, since both only have closes.

Chapter Four has two goals: to bring together some of the concepts addressed in the previous chapters and to touch on some of the more advanced trading concepts that are the focus of my other educational materials (as detailed in the conclusion on page 205).

SECTION ONE

Candle Chart Applications

Properly used, candle charts not only help improve profits, but they also assist in preserving capital. They do so by helping you avoid a potential losing trade or exiting a profitable trade early. Exhibit 4.1 shows an example of the latter. The dashed lines in Exhibit 4.1 show a resistance area near 135. A tall white candle pierces this resistance in early March. For those who were already long this index, this was a green light to remain

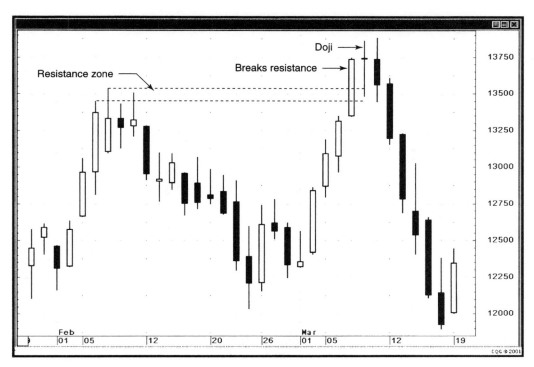

EXHIBIT 4.1   Oil Service Index: Daily (Using Candle Charts to Preserve Capital)
© CQG Inc. used by permission.

long. But observe what unfolded the next session—the doji. This doji line hinted that the bulls had lost full control of the market (however, it does not mean that the bears have taken control). With this doji, one should consider taking profits, moving up protective sell stops, or selling calls. This is a classic example of the power of candle charting techniques: Within one session we were able to glean the visual clue via the doji that while the market was maintaining its highs, the doji shouted that the bulls were not in complete control. So while the market looked healthy from the outside, the internals (as shown by the doji) were relaying the message that the market was not as healthy as it seemed. This market was, as the Japanese proverb states, "Like a leaking boat brightly painted."

A key concept is that the more technical signals that emerge at the same support or resistance level, the higher the likelihood of a reversal. This convergence concept can be applied with candles and Western techniques. That is, if a candle signal confirms a Western technical signal, as the Japanese proverb says, like the right hand helping the left. The charts in Exhibits 4.2

EXHIBIT 4.2 Semiconductor Index: Daily (Using Candle Charts to Confirm Resistance)

© Aspen Graphics. Used by permission.

and 4.3 are examples of the ease and power with which one can merge candle and Western charting techniques. Exhibit 4.2 shows how candles can confirm support and how we can use Western technical tools to get a price target. Exhibit 4.3 displays how a candle signal helped confirm a base.

Exhibit 4.2 shows how a gravestone doji helped reinforce a resistance zone near 420. Another technical signal at or near the same price area of the gravestone doji amplifies the candle signal's significance. As mentioned in Chapter One, a limitation of candle charts is that they normally don't provide price targets. This is why classic Western techniques, such as looking at support or resistance lines or pivot highs or lows, is so important, since you use these levels as targets. With this in mind, let's turn our attention to the same chart. Observe how this market was in a box range (discussed in Chapter One, Section Three) of about 420 to 370. Once the gravestone doji confirmed the top end of the box range at 420, a trader could consider selling short with that signal (with a stop over the top end of the box range) with a target to the bottom end of the box range near 370. This objective was quickly meet.

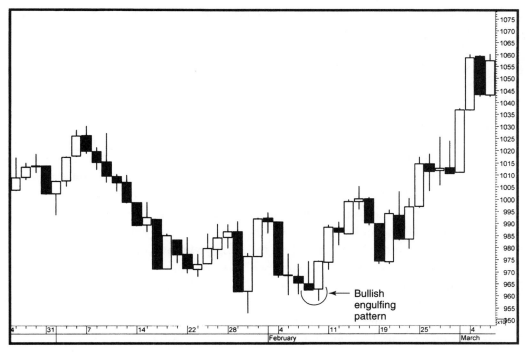

EXHIBIT 4.3 Dow Jones Industrials: Daily (Using Candle Charts to Confirm Support)

© Charts powered by MetaStock. Used by permission.

In Exhibit 4.3 a bullish engulfing pattern that took on extra importance as a turning signal is highlighted for two reasons. The first was that the lows of that bullish engulfing pattern confirmed a potential support level set by the lows made in late January. The second consideration is that, although a classic bullish engulfing pattern has a white candle wrapping around a prior black candle, this bullish engulfing pattern had a white candle that engulfed the three prior small real bodies (one of which was a doji). Though this aspect doesn't forecast that the market will move much higher than it would with a regular bullish engulfing pattern (remember, candles don't give targets), it does greatly improve the chances of a turn and thus makes a buy more attractive.

In the exhibits 4.2 and 4.3 I touched upon combining candle charting tools with Western technical analysis (please note that this book only touched the tip of the iceberg with this concept. Please see conclusion for more source material on ways to combine moving averages, volume, Bollinger bands, etc with candle charts).

Candle signals converge, just as Western technical indicators do. This means that if you see more than one candlestick signal confirming support or resistance set by another candle pattern, such as a hammer confirming a support area set by a bullish engulfing pattern, the likelihood of a turn increases. Exhibit 4.4 illustrates what I call a confluence of candles. This chart also shows that candle charting techniques are easily applicable to intraday charts.

Exhibit 4.4 shows a bearish falling window, or resistance zone, from $39.80 to $40.20. Thus, one could consider selling on a move up to that window. The stock got to that level at candle line A. But although the stock was at resistance, would one sell short with a tall white candle? I wouldn't recommend that, even if the market is at a resistance level! Notice what unfolded after candle line A: As shown at area B, the market formed a series of small real bodies (aka spinning tops). These small real bodies tell us that the bulls were tired, confirming the market's hesitation at the resistance zone set by the falling window. This could be a good time to sell short. Of course, if the market closed over the top of the falling window (i.e., $40.20), one should reconsider being short. As such we had one candle signal (the falling window) set the resistance area and another candle signal (the small real bodies) reinforcing that supply was stepping in at the window's resistance.

Because candle charts often send out reversal signals much sooner than bar charts, candles will shine at helping you improve market timing. Indeed, some of our advisory clients use fundamentals to decide which markets to buy or sell and then use the candles for timing these buy or sell times. Exhibit 4.5 illustrates how a trader might use the candles to enter or exit trades.

EXHIBIT 4.4 American Express: 60 minute (Confluence of Candles)

© Aspen Graphics. Used by permission.

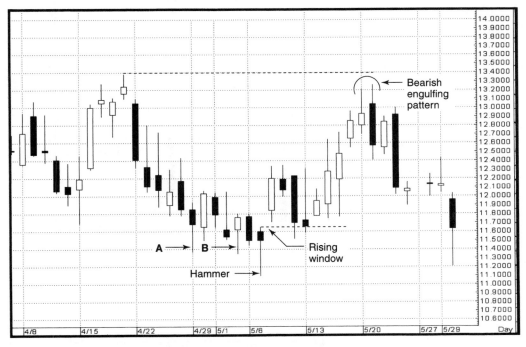

EXHIBIT 4.5 Converse Technology: Daily (Using Candle Signals to Enter or Exit Trades)

© Aspen Graphics. Used by permission.

A hammer forms on May 7 (the upper shadow was small enough to make this a hammer). This, in combination with the series of bullish shadows shown at A and B, was a strong indication that the market was trying to build a foundation for a rally. One could buy on that hammer with a stop under the low of the hammer. In the next session the market formed a rising window, which was another positive signal. A few days after this rising window the stock descended, but the bottom of the rising window maintained itself as support based on the close (remember that it takes a *close* under the bottom of a rising window for the window's support to be broken). Since this support held, we would stay long. In the week of May 13, the market moved north. The emergence of a bearish engulfing pattern near $13.30 at a resistance level defined by the highs of April 19 (shown by the dashed line) was a strong indication to take profits from the longs purchased on the hammer session.

In Exhibits 4.6A and 4.6B I show just one of the many ways a trader can harness the power of intraday candle charts to get a leg up on the competition.

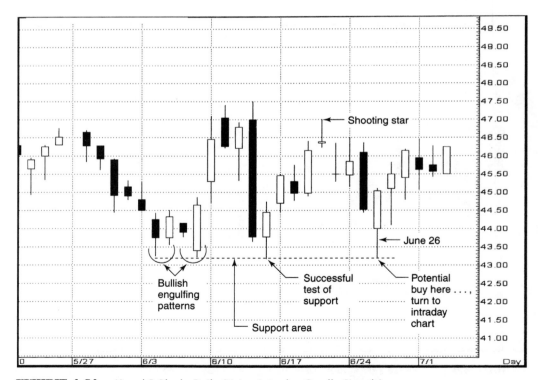

EXHIBIT 4.6A   H and R Block: Daily (Using Intraday Candle Signals)

EXHIBIT 4.6B H and R Block: 5 Minute (Using Intraday Candle Signals)

In Exhibit 4.6A we see a solid band of support near $43.25 underpinned by the dual bullish engulfing patterns on the week of June 3. The lows set by these two bullish engulfing patterns was successfully defended on June 14. The rally that began on June 14 stalled with a shooting star near $47. As the price dip from this shooting star approached the aforementioned support area toward $43.25 on June 26, you might consider buying on the session. To help improve our timing we can turn to an intraday chart to see if there are any buy signals as the stock approached $43.25 intraday. We now turn to the 5-minute chart of this stock at Exhibit 4.6B.

On this June 26 5-minute chart, the horizontal line shows the support area obtained from the daily chart (Exhibit 4.6a) near $43.25. This level was confirmed by a hammer. Therefore we can buy on that hammer based on this 5-minute chart because it confirmed a support level derived from the longer-term daily chart. These two exhibits illustrate the concept of using a longer time frame (daily) to obtain support or resistance and then a shorter time frame's candle signal (a 5-minute chart) to place the trade. This concept can be expanded to any two time frames. Thus, for example, you could use a weekly chart to get a support level and see if there are any bullish candle signals on a daily chart as the stock gets to this support.

SECTION TWO

Trading Guidelines

I n Section One of this chapter I gave some real-world examples so you could get a feel for how to apply the tools and techniques of Chapters One to Three. Now we take the next step by listing the pivotal trading concepts explained in the preceding chapters.

A note of caution: Market conditions affect some of the precepts listed below. According to one of the guidelines below, northern doji are normally more significant than southern doji. While this is generally true, if there's a southern doji confirming a major support area, you can be assured that I would pay close attention to that southern doji. This brings to the fore the importance of looking at all candle signals and trading guidelines in the context of the market environment.

THE GUIDELINES

- As the real body gets smaller, it implies that the prior trend is losing steam.
- The larger the real body, the greater the force underpinning the move.
- The more technical signals, whether Eastern (candles) or Western, that confirm the same support or resistance level, the greater the chance for a bounce from support or decline from resistance.
- Northern doji are normally more significant than southern doji.
- A series of long upper shadows as the market is ascending implies that the bulls do not have full control.
- A series of long lower shadows as the market is falling hints that the bears do not have full control.
- The rising and falling windows are, respectively, bullish and bearish continuation indicators.

- Doji in the middle of a box range are not a trading signal, since there is no trend to reverse.
- Candle charts are best used as a tool, not a system.
- Resistance or support is not considered broken unless by a close.
- If you see a reversal signal, consider initiating a new position only if that signal is in the direction of the major trend.
- Never place a trade with a candle signal until you have considered the risk/reward of the potential trade.
- Candle signals can denote areas of support and resistance.
- Candle indicators do not offer price targets.
- You should wait for the session's close to confirm a candle signal.
- A hanging man needs bearish confirmation by a close under the hanging man's real body.
- When analyzing a single candle line, one should consider both the real body and the shadows.
- Remember the importance of stops.
- The entire space of the rising window is a support area, with the most important area the bottom of the rising window.
- The entire area of the falling window is a resistance zone, with its most important area the top of the falling window.

CHAPTER FIVE

Progressive Charting

USING CANDLESTICK ANALYSIS

At my seminars one of the most frequent questions is, "What's the best way to get comfortable with candle charting techniques?" My reply is to print out a chart, place a blank piece of paper over the chart, and hide all the candle lines. Slide the blank piece of paper from left to right, revealing a single candle line, or a few candle lines, at a time. Looking at the exposed single candle lines (or a few candle lines) the student of candle charts asks, "What signal do I see and what are the market applications of the signal?"

To reinforce the material presented so far, we will do something similar—we will dissect a single market bit by bit. We will look at five months' worth of data on a candlestick chart, going a day or a few days at a time. One chart will be broken into 44 parts, with each part another day or a few days into the next time frame. For example, chart 3 has candle lines ending on June 15, and chart 4 has the same candle lines in chart 3 plus the next session's candle line.

The techniques discussed in the answer section are related to the ideas already presented in this book. Some of you who are very familiar with candles may see signals in the charts that are not addressed in the answers. This was done because some candle patterns and techniques are beyond the scope of this book. Nonetheless, even with these basic concepts, using this section will let you get up to speed quickly, harnessing the unique insights provided by candles.

For each of the 44 Exhibits, ask yourself these questions:

1. What candlestick signal do I see (if any)?
2. What are the potential implications of that signal?
3. How is this candlestick line related to the prior price action?
4. Are there any other aspects of recent or prior price action that are important?

At the end of this section I will give you my observations. These are denoted in Exhibits 5.45 to 5.88.

QUESTIONS

EXHIBIT 5.1   Question 5.1

EXHIBIT 5.2   Question 5.2

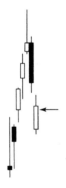

EXHIBIT 5.3   Question 5.3

EXHIBIT 5.4   Question 5.4

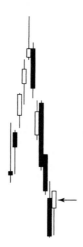

EXHIBIT 5.5   Question 5.5

EXHIBIT 5.6 Question 5.6

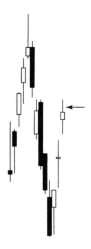

EXHIBIT 5.7 Question 5.7

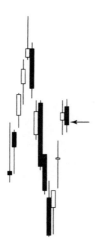

EXHIBIT 5.8   Question 5.8

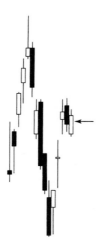

EXHIBIT 5.9   Question 5.9

EXHIBIT 5.10   Question 5.10

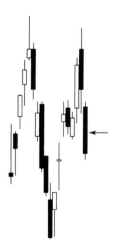

EXHIBIT 5.11   Question 5.11

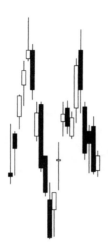

EXHIBIT 5.12   Question 5.12

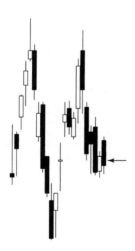

EXHIBIT 5.13   Question 5.13

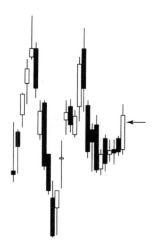

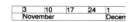

EXHIBIT 5.14   Question 5.14

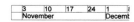

EXHIBIT 5.15   Question 5.15

EXHIBIT 5.16   Question 5.16

EXHIBIT 5.17   Question 5.17

3	10	17	24	1	8
November				December	

EXHIBIT 5.18   Question 5.18

3	10	17	24	1	8	15
November				December		

EXHIBIT 5.19   Question 5.19

EXHIBIT 5.20 Question 5.20

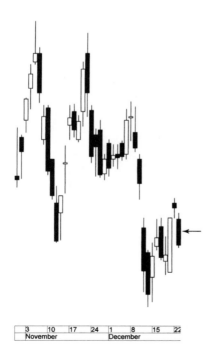

EXHIBIT 5.21 Question 5.21

EXHIBIT 5.22   Question 5.22

EXHIBIT 5.23   Question 5.23

EXHIBIT 5.24   Question 5.24

EXHIBIT 5.25   Question 5.25

EXHIBIT 5.26   Question 5.26

EXHIBIT 5.27   Question 5.27

EXHIBIT 5.28 Question 5.28

EXHIBIT 5.29 Question 5.29

EXHIBIT 5.30   Question 5.30

EXHIBIT 5.31   Question 5.31

EXHIBIT 5.32   Question 5.32

EXHIBIT 5.33   Question 5.33

EXHIBIT 5.34 Question 5.34

EXHIBIT 5.35 Question 5.35

EXHIBIT 5.36 Question 5.36

EXHIBIT 5.37 Question 5.37

EXHIBIT 5.38   Question 5.38

EXHIBIT 5.39   Question 5.39

EXHIBIT 5.40 Question 5.40

EXHIBIT 5.41 Question 5.41

EXHIBIT 5.42   Question 5.42

EXHIBIT 5.43   Question 5.43

EXHIBIT 5.44   Question 5.44

ANSWERS, OR MARKET OBSERVATIONS

In Exhibit 5.45, although the market was ascending, the extended upper shadow of the candle line at the arrow reflects that one of two things was happening: Either the bulls were retreating as the market approached the upper end of its daily range, or the bears had enough force to overwhelm the bulls. In either scenario the result is the same: a market whose rally had stalled as it approached the upper end of its trading range and then closed near the lows of that session. This candle line is a shooting star, which as the Japanese say, represents trouble overhead.

In Exhibit 5.46, the potential bearish applications of the shooting star were reinforced in this session with a long black real body that wrapped around the small white real body of the shooting star. The result was a bearish engulfing pattern. This reinforced the likelihood of a top (if the bulls had had enough wherewithal to push the market above the high of the shooting star, that would be a bullish breakout). I want to point out something interesting about this bearish engulfing pattern. When you see a bearish engulfing pattern, you may think it resembles a Western key reversal or outside day. A

EXHIBIT 5.45   Answer to Question 5.1

EXHIBIT 5.46   Answer to Question 5.2

key reversal day, or outside day, takes place when the market makes a new high during an uptrend. It then falls to close below the prior day's close, resulting in a bearish signal. With this bearish engulfing pattern, the second session that made up this pattern (i.e., the black candle) did not make a new high for the session. Therefore, if this was a bar chart, there would have been no reversal signal via an outside reversal session. All we need for the bearish engulfing pattern, however, is a black real body wrapping around a white real body, which occurred here. Consequently, we were able to obtain a bearish reversal signal on the candlestick chart that was not available on a traditional bar chart.

In Exhibit 5.47, a small falling window adds further bearish applications to the bearish engulfing pattern. Although it's a small falling window (with windows, size doesn't matter), this window now represents a potential resistance area.

In Exhibit 5.48, the falling window's resistance level was confirmed with a long black real body. Although there is a black real body wrapping around a white real body, this was not a bearish engulfing pattern. The reason is that a bearish engulfing pattern comes after an ascent, not during a decline, as was the case here. Although this was not a bearish engulfing pattern, the

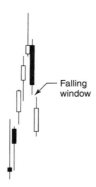

— Falling window

EXHIBIT 5.47   Answer to Question 5.3

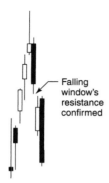

Falling window's resistance confirmed

3   1
Novemb

EXHIBIT 5.48   Answer to Question 5.4

fact that there was an extended black real body does further damage to the technical picture.

In Exhibit 5.49, for a few sessions after the long black real body, the market continued its descent. The small real body white candle shown here, with its extended lower shadow, does take some bearish steam out of the market because of the bullish shadow. In addition, it was a successful retest of the prior session's low, forming a tweezers bottom. This candle line, although constructive because of its extended lower shadow, is not a hammer. Why? Because for a hammer the lower shadow must be at least two times the height of the real body. This lower shadow did not meet that criterion.

A rally during the next session came by way of a small rising window and a high wave candle. The high wave candle, with its extended upper lower shadows and small real body, lessens the bullish applications of the rally. However, there was not a major trend to reverse, so we should not view this as a strong bearish reversal signal since the market was not overbought and hence not vulnerable. The real body of this candle line in Exhibit 5.50 was so small that we can also view it as a doji, and so it can also be called a high wave doji.

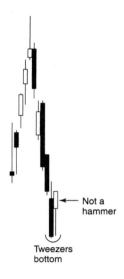

3   10
November

EXHIBIT 5.49   Answer to Question 5.5

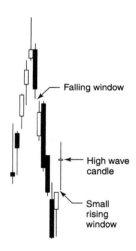

3   10
November

EXHIBIT 5.50   Answer to Question 5.6

The rally continues in Exhibit 5.51 with another rising window (rising window 2) and another high wave candle. This high wave candle has slightly more ominous implications than the prior high wave candle because the market is now at a resistance area, as defined by the falling window from the prior week. Consequently, we look for support at the rising window at 2 and resistance at the falling window.

In Exhibit 5.52, a black real body wrapping around the white real body forms a bearish engulfing pattern (this was a bearish engulfing pattern because the prior trend was up). While this bearish engulfing pattern is confirming the falling window's resistance, the market is still holding the support defined by rising window 2.

The market remains entrenched in a "battle of windows" in Exhibit 5.53 as the falling window remains resistance and the rising window is confirmed as support via the white candle. The white candle in the prior black real body looks like a piercing pattern, but it is not. This is because a piercing pattern as a bottom reversal signal must come after a downtrend. Instead, this candle came after an up/lateral market.

Here is a rally followed immediately by a black real body that opens above the prior session's high and closes more than midway into the prior

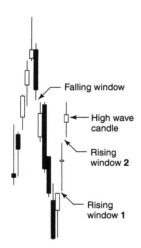

Falling window

High wave candle

Rising window 2

Rising window 1

EXHIBIT 5.51   Answer to Question 5.7

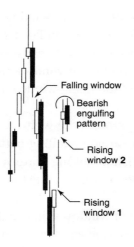

Falling window

Bearish
engulfing
pattern

Rising
window **2**

Rising
window **1**

3 | 10 | 17
November

EXHIBIT 5.52   Answer to Question 5.8

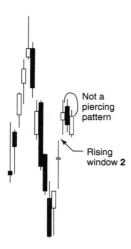

Not a
piercing
pattern

Rising
window **2**

3 | 10 | 17
November

EXHIBIT 5.53   Answer to Question 5.9

white real body, forming a dark cloud cover. This bearish signal in Exhibit 5.54 is not surprising since the dark cloud cover emerged at the resistance level set by the bearish engulfing pattern built a few weeks earlier. On the flip side, we could look for support at rising window 2.

The close under the support at rising window 2 now means that the next potential support area is at rising window 1 in Exhibit 5.55.

Over the next few sessions the market began stabilizing above the support set at the rising window. At the last two candle lines shown in Exhibit 5.56, there was a white real body closing into a prior black real body. However, this was not a classic piercing pattern because the close of the white real body should be above the middle of the black real body (shown by the dashed line). Although this is not a classic piercing pattern, because this was the first white candle in five sessions, and this white candle held the lows of the prior two sessions, we get a sense that the market is trying to build a base.

In Exhibit 5.57 The market is expanding on the base detailed in Exhibit 5.56 above.

In Exhibit 5.58 a tall white candle that penetrates a resistance area set by the last four sessions puts the bulls back in control. An earlier indication that

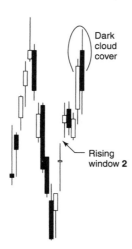

EXHIBIT 5.54   Answer to Question 5.10

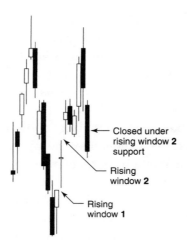

Closed under
rising window **2**
support

Rising
window **2**

Rising
window **1**

3   10   17
November

EXHIBIT 5.55   Answer to Question 5.11

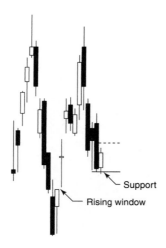

Support

Rising window

3   10   17   24
November

EXHIBIT 5.56   Answer to Question 5.12

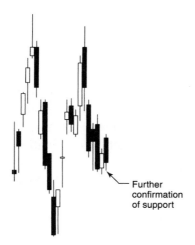

EXHIBIT 5.57   Answer to Question 5.13

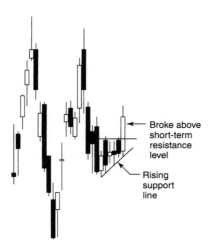

EXHIBIT 5.58   Answer to Question 5.14

the bulls were gaining some momentum came with the series of mostly higher lows preceding this tall white candle, displayed as a rising support line. This formed an ascending triangle that showed that the buyers were more eager to buy on price dips. This ascending triangle brings outs a vital element about candle charts: They can use any technique that can be used on a bar chart, because the candle chart uses the same open, high, low, and close data as a bar chart. Indeed, I strongly recommend merging traditional Western technical analysis with candle charts. Such a combination will further enhance the power of your analysis.

While the rising support line is still in force in Exhibit 5.59, the high wave candle gives us a sense that the upside drive might be losing some momentum. The new high close for this move on the high wave candle session keeps the short-term trend mostly positive, in spite of the high wave candle. For bearish confirmation of this particular high wave candle, there should be a close under the real body of the candle to confirm that the bears have taken over.

In Exhibit 5.60 we got the bearish confirmation detailed in question 15. This session, when combined with the prior two sessions, forms a classic evening star pattern. Although this is a bearish pattern, selling short here would not have an attractive risk/reward profile because the market is still holding that rising support line. Therefore, if you sell on the close of the black real body, you are selling at support. (The critical concepts of risk/ reward and money-management techniques are discussed in detail in my other products as described in the conclusion section.)

In Exhibit 5.61, the market opened a gap under the rising support line. For those familiar with classic Western technical tools, a gap under a support or resistance area is called a breakaway gap. (Remember that the terms gap and window are synonymous.) This breakaway gap, or falling window, should become resistance since a falling window is resistance. Although this breakaway gap is now resistance, we still have the rising window from the prior month as support.

Another gap down (i.e., a falling window) and a new low close for the move puts the bears in control in Exhibit 5.62.

As shown in Exhibit 5.63, after a period of some stabilization in the middle of December, the market rallied and then stalled at the falling window via a bearish engulfing pattern. Remember that the whole window is potential resistance. As such, the resistance can begin at the bottom of the falling window, as it did here.

Although the entire space of a falling window is resistance, the most critical area of resistance for a falling window is at the top of a falling window.

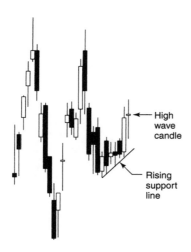

High
wave
candle

Rising
support
line

3	10	17	24	1	
November				Decemb	

EXHIBIT 5.59 Answer to Question 5.15

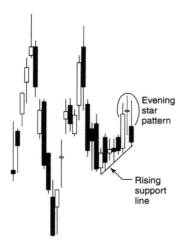

Evening
star
pattern

Rising
support
line

3	10	17	24	1	8
November				Decembe	

EXHIBIT 5.60 Answer to Question 5.16

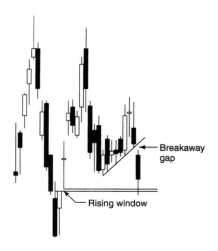

EXHIBIT 5.61   Answer to Question 5.17

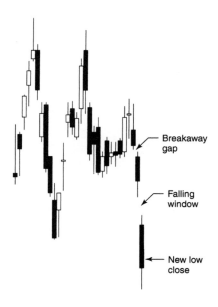

EXHIBIT 5.62   Answer to Question 5.18

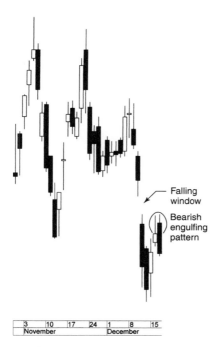

Falling window

Bearish engulfing pattern

| 3 | 10 | 17 | 24 | 1 | 8 | 15 |
November / December

EXHIBIT 5.63 Answer to Question 5.19

Consequently, in spite of the new high close for this move on this candle line in Exhibit 5.64, its small real body hints that the top of the falling window would maintain itself as resistance.

With the candle line in Exhibit 5.65, we now have an evening star pattern. Although this is a bearish turning signal, especially since it confirmed a falling window's resistance, we still have to look at the rising support line as a potential support area. Thus, if you sold at the third session of this evening star (that is, the session that completes this pattern), you'd be selling at a potential support area. Once again we see the overwhelming importance of thinking about the risk/reward aspect of a trade based on a candle signal.

Although the market has been ascending along the slope set by the rising support line in Exhibit 5.66, it is now at a pivotal resistance area defined by the top of the falling window. Since this is such a tight support/resistance range over the next day or two, one of these levels should be breached. Either we will see a break above the top of the falling window, which would be a bullish signal, or a close under the ascending support line, which would be a bearish signal.

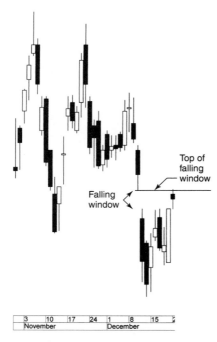

EXHIBIT 5.64 Answer to Question 5.20

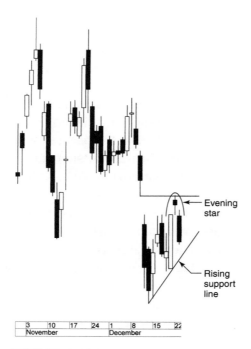

EXHIBIT 5.65 Answer to Question 5.21

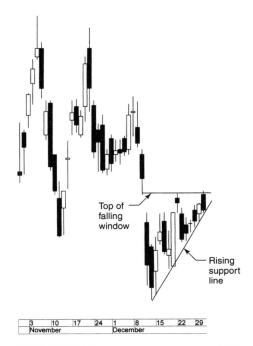

Top of falling window

Rising support line

3   10   17   24   1   8   15   22   29
November   December

EXHIBIT 5.66   Answer to Question 5.22

In Exhibit 5.67 the market was propelled higher via a tall white candle, shattering the falling window's resistance level. In spite of the tall white real body, the stock is now near a potential resistance area defined by the breakaway gap (which is the same as a falling window) from early December. As such, one should be cautious about buying at this session's close, because doing so would mean buying at a resistance level.

Now Exhibit 5.68 shows a tug-of-war between the rising support line as a floor and the breakaway gap as a ceiling. This action shows us a powerful advantage of the candle charts in that they can help preserve capital. As detailed in question 5.23, although on the prior tall white candle session the market may have looked healthy, we would likely not have gone long because this white candle was near a resistance area set by the breakaway gap. Thus, using candle charting techniques (aka the breakaway gap as resistance) keeps us from prematurely going long and thus avoid a potentially losing trade. Properly used candles will help you preserve capital.

Once again this market gapped down under a support area, forming another breakaway gap, as shown in Exhibit 5.69. This now becomes resistance.

Breakaway gap

Closed over window's resistance level

Rising support line

3   10   17   24   1   8   15   22   29   5
November   December   Ja

EXHIBIT 5.67   Answer to Question 5.23

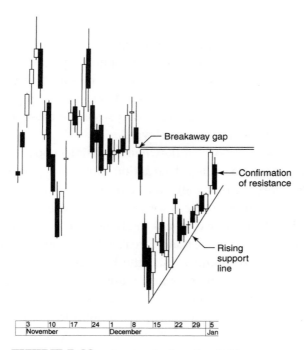

Breakaway gap

Confirmation of resistance

Rising support line

3   10   17   24   1   8   15   22   29   5
November   December   Jan

EXHIBIT 5.68   Answer to Question 5.24

Gap under support (breakaway gap)

EXHIBIT 5.69 Answer to Question 5.25

Exhibit 5.70 confirms the resistance area set by the breakaway gap discussed in question 5.25. This candle line, with its long upper shadow and small real body near the bottom end of the trading range, has the same configuration as the shooting star. But a shooting star must come after an uptrend. This candle came after a short-term downtrend and thus would not be called a shooting star. However, its long upper shadow and close near the lower end of the session does have bearish implications.

A bullish counterattack pattern emerged in Exhibit 5.71 as the market opened sharply lower than the prior session's close and then bounced back to close at the prior session's close. This is a strong implication that the bulls were starting to grab control of the market from the bears. This bullish counterattack pattern has extra significance because it's helping confirm a support area defined by the mid-December lows.

The rally after the counterattack pattern is stalling at the falling window's resistance level in Exhibit 5.72. Therefore, we would need a close above the top of the falling window to show that the bulls are in control.

On this session in Exhibit 5.73, the market propelled itself above the falling window's resistance area and is now approaching potential resistance defined by the most recent high in early January.

EXHIBIT 5.70   Answer to Question 5.26

EXHIBIT 5.71   Answer to Question 5.27

EXHIBIT 5.72   Answer to Question 5.28

EXHIBIT 5.73   Answer to Question 5.29

EXHIBIT 5.74   Answer to Question 5.30

As we see in Exhibit 5.74, the market retreated from the potential resistance area set in early January. However, since the lows of the past few sessions are nearly the same, we get a sense that the market was trying build a base for a potential rally. This potential was further enhanced by the completion of the bullish engulfing pattern when the white real body wrapped around the black real body. While the market was building a floor, if you went long, you should remember that a close under this support area set by the past couple days would be viewed as a bearish signal. Using stops is a vital element in any trading plan.

The rally from the bullish engulfing pattern discussed in Exhibit 5.74 is stalling at a falling resistance line obtained by connecting the highs from late December and mid-January in Exhibit 5.75. A harami pattern (in which a small real body—in this case almost a doji—is within a prior long real body) reinforced the significance of this falling resistance line.

In Exhibit 5.76 the market gapped over the resistance area set by the falling resistance line detailed in Exhibit 5.75 above. This opened a bullish rising window. With the action, any of the potential bearish applications of the harami in Exhibit 5.75 are negated. With this rising window as potential sup-

EXHIBIT 5.75   Answer to Question 5.31

EXHIBIT 5.76   Answer to Question 5.32

port, where do we have potential resistance? For that we turn to the early December high at the top of the evening star.

The high wave candle stalling near the resistance area from early December shows us that the market is now confused in Exhibit 5.77. However, the new high close for the move on that session keeps the trend slightly positive.

The hint that the high wave candle was signaling a potential reversal failed to materialize as the rally pushed this market above a resistance area in Exhibit 5.78. The upper shadow of this white real body slightly offset some of its bullish impact. This could be a very small sign of the warning that the market might be having some trouble as it approaches the major resistance set by the dark cloud cover in mid-November.

The black real body in Exhibit 5.79 completed a bearish dark cloud cover. For potential support we could look to the rising window from early February. Keep in mind that although there is a rising window, that does not necessarily mean the market will be drawn like a magnet to that window's potential support area.

The black real body shown in Exhibit 5.80 wrapping around the prior white real body is not a bearish engulfing pattern. Although this combination of candle lines is correct for a bearish engulfing pattern, these two lines came

3	10	17	24	1	8	15	22	29	5	12	20	26	2
November				December					January				Fe

EXHIBIT 5.77   Answer to Question 5.33

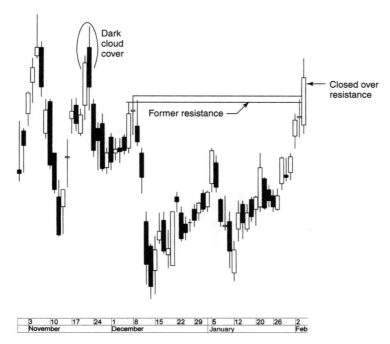

EXHIBIT 5.78　Answer to Question 5.34

EXHIBIT 5.79　Answer to Question 5.35

Not a bearish
engulfing pattern

| 3 | 10 | 17 | 24 | 1 | 8 | 15 | 22 | 29 | 5 | 12 | 20 | 26 | 2 | 5 |
| November | | | | December | | | | | January | | | | Februar | |

EXHIBIT 5.80   Answer to Question 5.36

after a decline. As we know, a bearish engulfing pattern must come after a rally for it to be a top reversal signal.

A series of white real bodies in the last two sessions and the market's mostly higher highs and higher lows over the last week keeps the short-term trend up in Exhibit 5.81. However, it is now approaching a resistance area set by the dark cloud cover.

The appearance of the bearish engulfing pattern that was completed on the black real body in Exhibit 5.82 reinforced the importance of the resistance at the dark cloud cover.

In Exhibit 5.83, another bearish engulfing pattern adds onto a top built by the prior bearish engulfing pattern and dark cloud cover. However, a support area defined by the lows of the lows of the prior five sessions is holding. This puts the market in a box range.

The black candle on the session shown in Exhibit 5.84 breaks a multi-week support level. The bears are now in control.

In Exhibit 5.85 a falling window is now potential resistance. Thus far, the late January rising window is now next potential support. While this candle line has the same shape as a shooting star, it is not classified as such because it came after a decline rather than a rally.

EXHIBIT 5.81 Answer to Question 5.37

EXHIBIT 5.82 Answer to Question 5.38

EXHIBIT 5.83 Answer to Question 5.39

EXHIBIT 5.84 Answer to Question 5.40

Falling window

Not a shooting star

EXHIBIT 5.85 Answer to Question 5.41

The black candle broke the rising window's support level in Exhibit 5.86. A point to remember is that once a window's support level is breached, that window is voided. In other words, if the market rallies after the break of the window's support and comes back to the broken window's support, that window should no longer be viewed as support. With the current candle line, the market, on the plus side, opens a small rising window. On the negative side, this candle line stalled at the falling window's resistance. With such tight support and resistance, the market should break out one way or the other in a day or two.

The candle in Exhibit 5.87 shows that the break was to the downside as the prior session's rising window was breached. Notice how the high of this black candle stopped at the falling window's resistance.

In Exhibit 5.88, this session's bearish shadow once again highlights the significance of the falling window's resistance.

EXHIBIT 5.86 Answer to Question 5.42

EXHIBIT 5.87 Answer to Question 5.43

EXHIBIT 5.88 Answer to Question 5.45

CHAPTER SIX

Bringing It All Together: Real-World Charts

T his is where we bring it all together. The pages that follow give you an opportunity to take advantage of interactive workshop material, including real-world, hands-on practice charts. Through working with them, you will apply what you've learned in this course book. The goal of this section is to provide a mechanism to determine your level of comfort with candle charts, and the detailed answers help to further refine your knowledge.

The charts show that while candle signals give valuable timing tools for entering and exiting the markets, they are not 100% accurate. A chart might show, for example, a bullish harami pattern with the market falling after the emergence of that bullish signal. This is why stops are so important. My goal is getting you comfortable with recognizing the patterns—even if they don't work as forecast.

In this chapter you will learn . . .

- How to determine support and resistance levels for rising and falling windows
- How to determine the risk/reward aspects of a potential trade
- To know when to stand aside and when to initiate a trade
- How to tell if a trend is gaining or losing force
- To name candle patterns on a chart
- How to obtain bearish and bullish confirmation for a candle signal
- The importance of viewing candle signals within market context

- The importance of multiple layers of confirmation for support or resistance
- The importance of trend in determining a candle signal

Key terms to watch for:

- Bullish engulfing pattern
- Dragonfly
- Falling window
- Hammer
- Harami
- Morning star
- Northern doji
- Resistance
- Shooting star
- Southern doji
- Support

CHECK YOUR UNDERSTANDING

Questions for Chapter Six: Bringing It All Together: Real-World Charts

Use Exhibit 6.1 for questions 1 and 2.

1. For areas A, B, and C, which is a rising window? A falling window?

2. What are their respective support and resistance zones?

Use Exhibit 6.2 to answer questions 3 to 7.

3. Highlight the three rising windows before candle line A on March 22.

4. Based on these rising windows, where would support levels be? If the first support at the top rising window was broken, where would we expect next support?

5. What is the candle line at X?

6. If one buys at line X, where is a potential resistance area? (hint: Connect highs from A and B.)

7. Based on the question above, would a buy on the close of line X present an attractive risk/reward profile?

Use Exhibit 6.3 for questions 8 to 10.

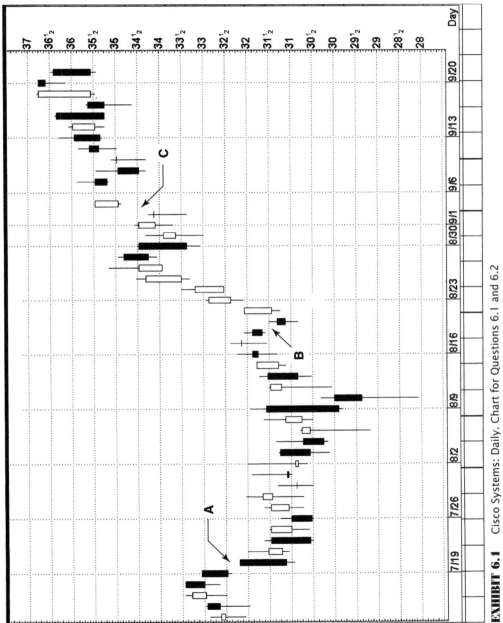

EXHIBIT 6.1   Cisco Systems: Daily. Chart for Questions 6.1 and 6.2

© Aspen Graphics. Used by permission.

179

180

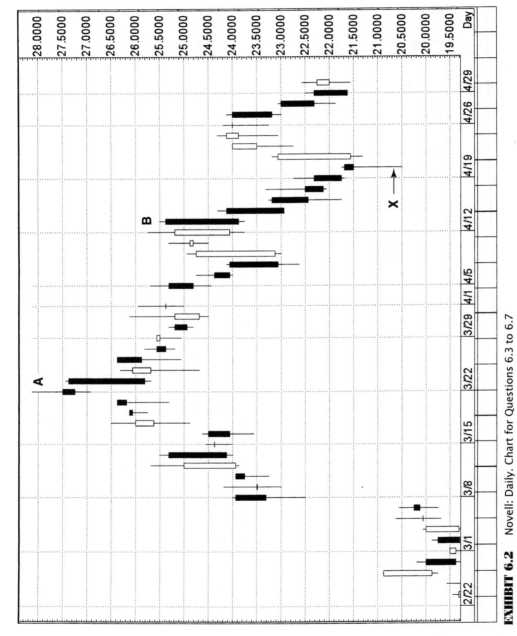

EXHIBIT 6.2 Novell: Daily. Chart for Questions 6.3 to 6.7

© Aspen Graphics. Used by permission.

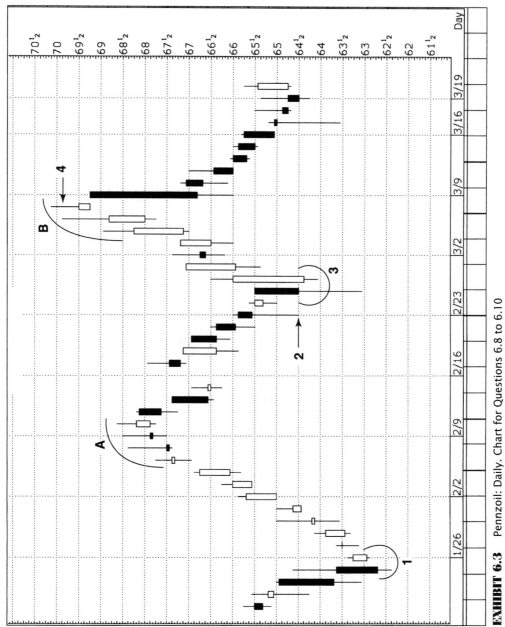

EXHIBIT 6.3 Pennzoil: Daily. Chart for Questions 6.8 to 6.10

© Aspen Graphics. Used by permission.

8. What are the candle signals at 1, 2, 3, and 4?

9. At area A, how were the candle lines hinting that the market was losing bullish momentum even though the stock was making higher highs and higher closes?

10. In early March (area B) the stock made another series of higher highs and higher closes. What were the candlesticks hinting about the extent of the bulls' control?

Use Exhibit 6.4 to answer questions 11 and 12.

11. Name the four candlestick signals at 1, 2, 3, and 4 that underscore support near $75.

12. What happened at signal 5 that gave this market a further bullish outlook?

Use Exhibit 6.5 to answer questions 13 to 18.

13. Highlight the rising windows.

14. What are the candle signals at X and Y?

15. Is X a potentially bearish signal? Why or why not?

16. Would you sell on the close of line X? (Hint: Note X's low and the prior session's high.)

17. What would be bearish confirmation of the potential negative candlestick signal line at X?

18. What would cause us to reassess a bearish view based on signal Y?

Use Exhibit 6.6 to answer questions 19 to 21.

19. What are the patterns at A and B?

20. What were the two aspects that made pattern B more likely a bottom reversal?

21. After the week of October 8, why was there support near $23?

Use Exhibit 6.7 for questions 22 to 24.

22. What were the signals at A, B, and C?

23. Highlight the harami patterns on this chart.

24. What was especially significant about the two candle lines at C?

Use Exhibit 6.8 to answer question 25.

25. Which of the numbered lines are hammers?

Use Exhibit 6.9 for questions 26 to 28.

26. What signals at 1, 2, and 3 show hesitation near the 1970/1975 area?

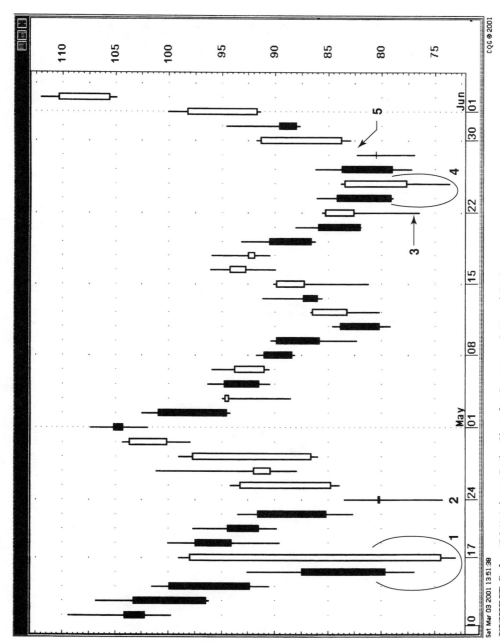

EXHIBIT 6.4 JDS Uniphase: Daily. Chart for Questions 6.11 and 6.12

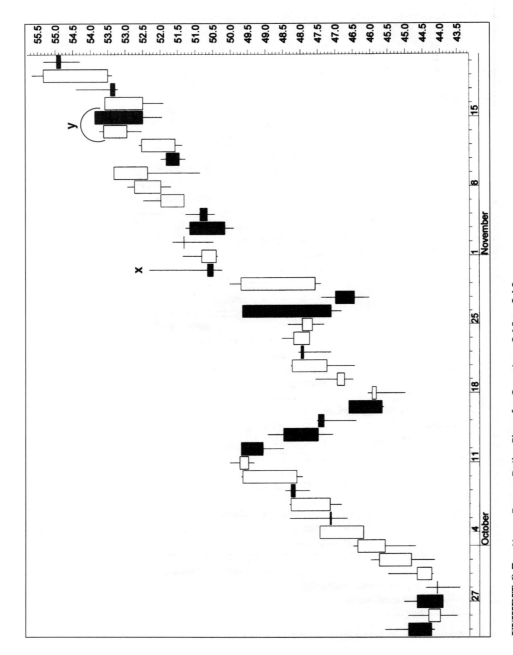

EXHIBIT 6.5   Home Depot: Daily. Chart for Questions 6.13 to 6.18

© Charts powered by MetaStock. Used by permission.

184

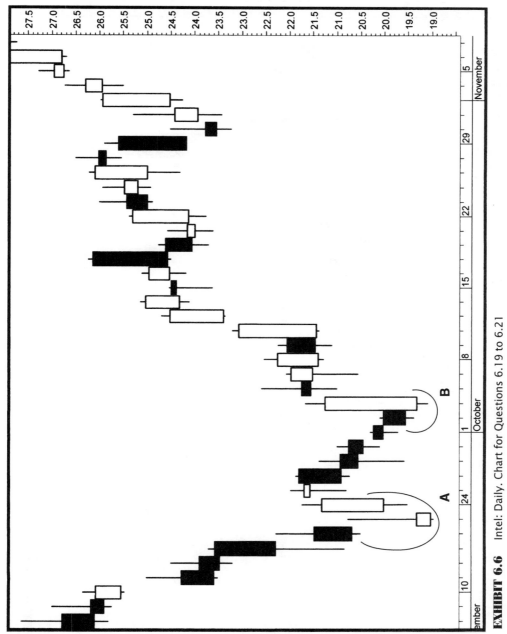

EXHIBIT 6.6 Intel: Daily. Chart for Questions 6.19 to 6.21

© Charts powered by MetaStock. Used by permission.

185

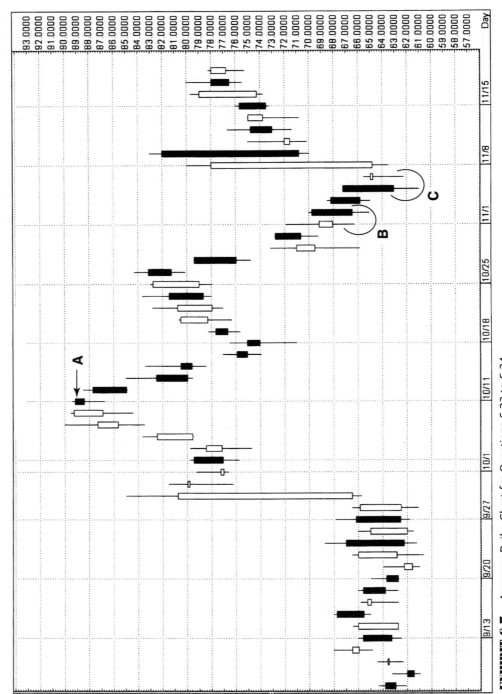

EXHIBIT 6.7 Amazon: Daily. Chart for Questions 6.22 to 6.24

© Aspen Graphics. Used by permission.

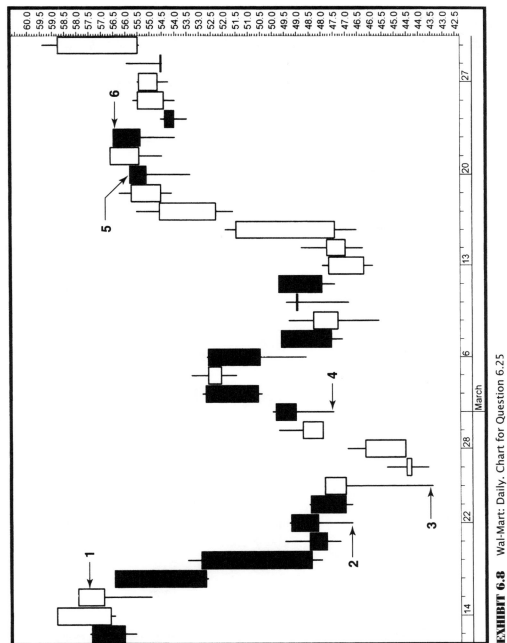

EXHIBIT 6.8 Wal-Mart: Daily. Chart for Question 6.25

© Charts powered by MetaStock. Used by permission.

187

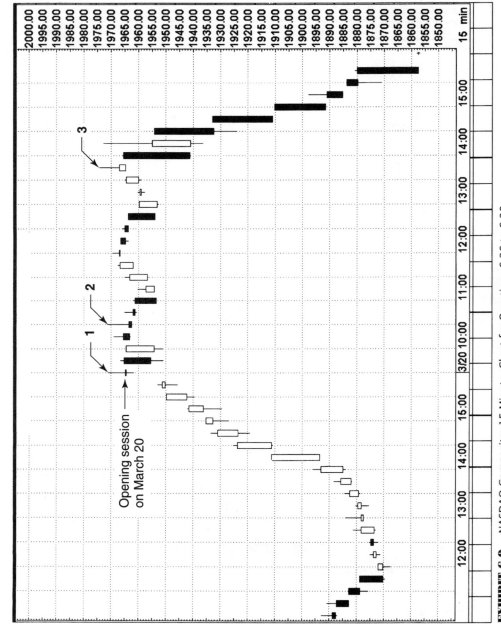

EXHIBIT 6.9 NASDAQ Composite: 15 Minute. Chart for Questions 6.26 to 6.28

© Aspen Graphics. Used by permission.

188

27. After the opening on March 20 (at candle line 1), why is there support near 1950?

28. While the doji at 1 suggested that the market was tired, what was needed to confirm its potentially bearish implications? (Hint: See question 2.)

Use Exhibit 6.10 to answer questions 29 to 42.

Match the list of candle signals below with the numbered candle lines and patterns in Exhibit 6.10.

29. Candle signals 1 are _____ .

30. Candle signal 2 is a _____ .

31. Candle signal 3 is a _____ .

32. Candle signal 4 is a _____ .

33. Candle signal 5 is a _____ .

34. Candle signal 6 is a _____ .

35. Candle signal 7 is a _____ .

36. Candle signal 8 is a _____ .

37. Candle signal 9 is a _____ .

38. Candle signal 10 is a _____ .

39. Candle signal 11 is a _____ .

40. Candle signal 12 is a _____ .

41. Candle signal 13 is a _____ .

42. Candle signal 14 is a _____ .

    a. bullish engulfing pattern

    b. bullish harami

    c. bearish harami

    d. falling window

    e. southern doji

    f. morning star

    g. northern doji

    h. shooting star

    i. hammer

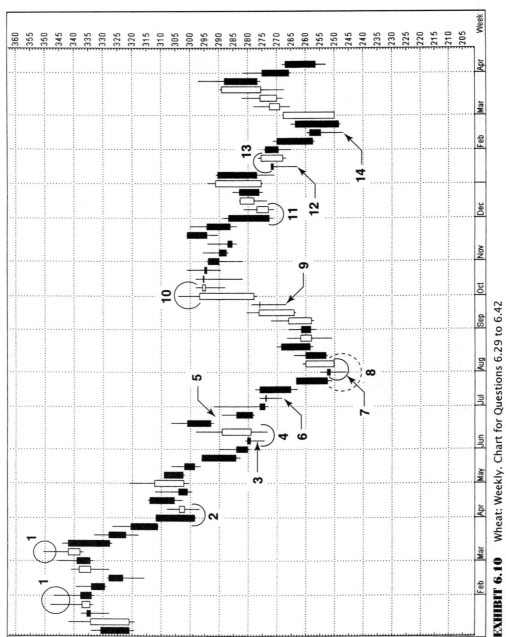

EXHIBIT 6.10 Wheat: Weekly. Chart for Questions 6.29 to 6.42

© Aspen Graphics. Used by permission.

Answers for Chapter Six: Bringing It All Together: Real-World Charts

1. There was a small falling window on July 20 at A (Exhibit 6.11; the dashed lines representing a resistance zone). Note how the market stalled near this window's resistance starting in late in July with a series of long upper shadow candles. There was a small falling window at B. The close on August 23 pushed the stock above the window's resistance area and, as a Japanese expression goes, "blew away the dirt."

2. A relatively large rising window unfolded between the sessions of September 2 and 3 (at C). A few sessions later (September 8) the market broke under the top of this window (near $35), but the bottom of the window near $34.25 remained as support. It would take a close under that level to confirm a break of support. This is based on the concept that a window's support is in force until the bears can close the market under the bottom of the window.

3. The three rising windows are shown in Exhibit 6.12.

4. Each of these rising windows is support, that is, the whole zone of the rising window. Consequently, when the market closed under the rising window 1 (on March 23) our next potential support area is rising window 2. The bottom of rising window 2 held as support for a few weeks, at least until the market closed under it on April 6. Once the bears broke the support at rising window 2, the next potential support area was defined by rising window 3 (from $22.50 to $20.50). The challenge with a large rising window like this is that it gives such a large potential support zone. Therefore, we don't have a tight potential support area, since the whole window is theoretically a support zone. Nonetheless, if we remember that the most important support of a rising window is the bottom of the window, we can focus our attention on potential pivotal support near the bottom of rising window 3, at $20.50.

5. The candle line at X is a hammer. This hammer takes on extra positive implications since it is a successful test of the bottom of a large window (3) at $20.50.

6. A limitation of candle charts is that they do not give price targets. Therefore, we shift to the Western technicals to obtain a potential price target. We can connect the highs at A and B to draw a falling resistance line. As a resistance area, it becomes our potential target on any bounces from the bullish hammer.

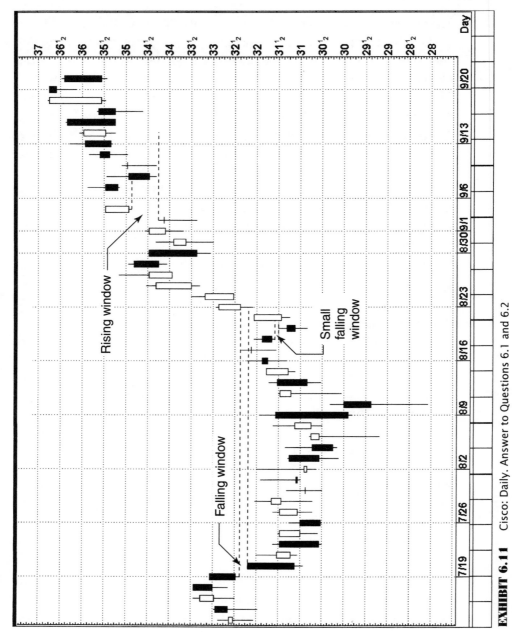

EXHIBIT 6.11 Cisco: Daily. Answer to Questions 6.1 and 6.2

© Aspen Graphics. Used by permission.

192

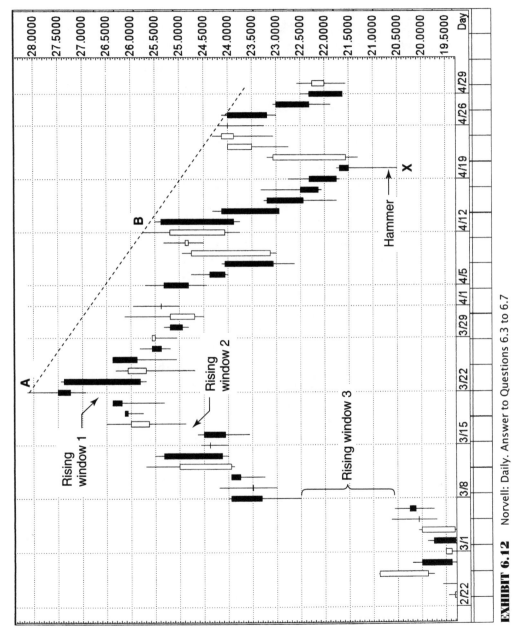

EXHIBIT 6.12 Norvell: Daily. Answer to Questions 6.3 to 6.7

© Aspen Graphics. Used by permission.

193

7. In this case buying at the hammer's close presents an attractive risk/reward profile since the risk is to the bottom of the hammer (about a $1 risk) for a potential target to the falling resistance line discussed above, near $24. This gives us a $2.50 upside target. Therefore, in this scenario the risk/reward is 1 to 2.50.

8. As shown in Exhibit 6.13, candle signal 1 is a harami, 2 is a hammer, 3 is a bullish engulfing pattern, and 4 a shooting star.

9. For area A, although the stock is making higher highs, higher lows, and higher closes, we're getting definite warning signs that the bulls are losing upside force based on the long upper shadows and small real bodies.

10. For area B, once again the market is making higher highs, higher lows, and higher closes. But the long upper shadows show that the bulls cannot hold the highs into the close of these sessions. Our final cautionary signal emerges at the shooting star.

11. In Exhibit 6.14, signal 1 is a bullish engulfing pattern. The height of the white real body that completed the bullish engulfing pattern would likely not present an attractive risk/reward since the market moved so far off its lows by the time the bullish pattern was completed. At signal 2 we see a doji confirming the potential support area defined by the bottom of the bullish engulfing pattern. Normally a doji in a downtrend (that is, a Southern doji) is not a potent bottom reversal signal. However in this scenario, since the doji confirms a pivotal support area, this Southern doji is a signal to watch. Signal 3 is a bullish hammer. Note how the low of this hammer became support based on a close. Signal 4 is a piercing pattern. The market is in a downtrend, and then we have a black real body, followed in the next session by a white real body that pushes deeply into a prior black real body.

12. Underscoring the importance of this support area defined by the aforementioned bullish candlestick signals, the market opened a small rising window giving further bullish impetus.

13. There are two rising windows, one in mid-October and the other in late October, as shown in Exhibit 6.15.

14. X is a shooting star (the lower shadow is small enough for this to be considered a shooting star). The candlestick signal at Y is a bearish engulfing pattern.

15. Yes, normally a shooting star is a potentially bearish signal due to its long upper shadow and close near the bottom end of the session's range.

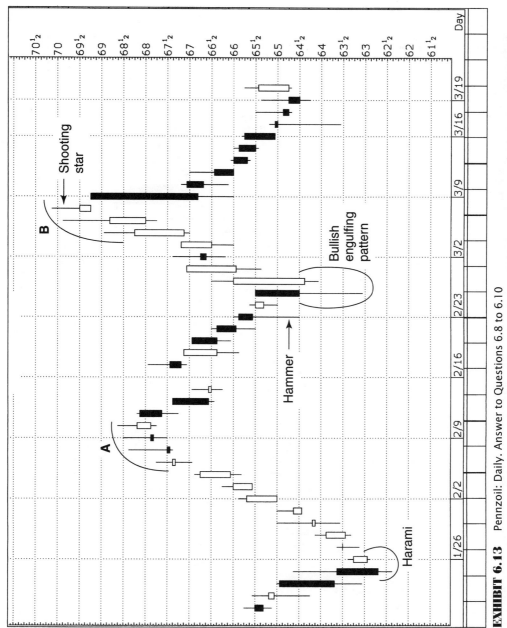

EXHIBIT 6.13 Pennzoil: Daily. Answer to Questions 6.8 to 6.10

© Aspen Graphics. Used by permission.

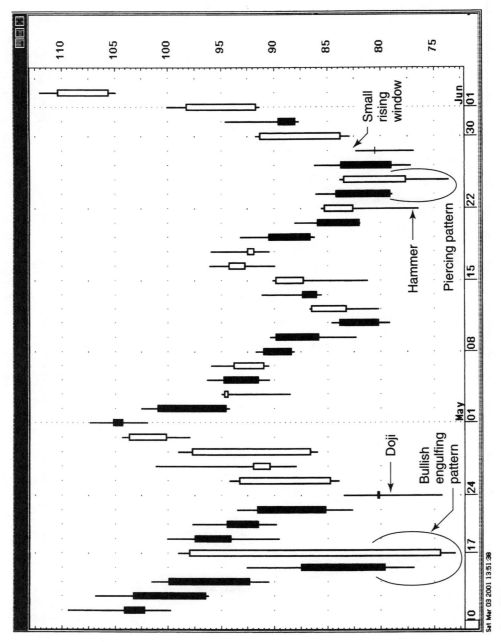

EXHIBIT 6.14 JDS Uniphase: Daily. Answer to Questions 6.11 and 6.12

© CQG Inc. Used by permission.

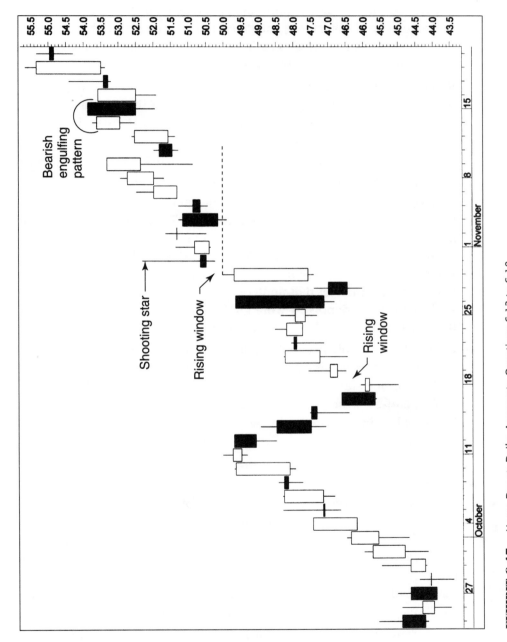

EXHIBIT 6.15 Home Depot: Daily. Answer to Questions 6.13 to 6.18

© Charts powered by MetaStock. Used by permission.

16. On the session of the shooting star mentioned in answer 15, the market opened a rising window. Therefore we received a bearish reversal signal (via a shooting star) at a support area (as defined by the rising window). Consequently, the shooting star would not be an attractive short sale based on the risk/reward aspect of the trade. This is because if you sell at this shooting star's close, you are selling near a support area.

17. Remembering the concept that a rising window should become support, to validate the potentially bearish implications of the shooting star, we would need a close under the rising window's support area. The support area is shown by the dashed line.

18. For signal Y, the bearish engulfing pattern, once the market closed above the high of that pattern it would be viewed as a break of resistance.

19. As shown at A in Exhibit 6.16, there is a morning star pattern, or more exactly, a variation on the classic morning star. This is because the classic morning star has as its first candle a long black real body rather than this average-sized black real body. Nonetheless, with the intrusion of the white real body (the third session of this pattern) deeply into this black real body, and the fact that none of the real bodies of this three candlestick pattern overlapped, I would still view it as a morning star. At B, there is a classic bullish engulfing pattern.

20. Pattern B was a bullish engulfing pattern and the two aspects that made this pattern more significant were (1) that it was successful confirmation of the morning star's support and (2) that the white real body of the engulfing pattern wrapped around not only one black real body, but four black real bodies (as shown by the dashed lines).

21. The support level engendered during the week of October 8 was due to a very small rising window (upper dashed lines).

22. Signal A (Exhibit 6.17) was a hanging man, which was confirmed in the next session (for the bearish implications of a hanging man to be confirmed we need to close under the hanging man's close the next session). Signal B was not a bearish engulfing pattern. Although the combination of candle lines was correct, that is a black real body covering a white real body. A bearish engulfing pattern must come after an uptrend, not a downtrend, as in this example. Signal C was a harami pattern, because a small real body was contained in an unusually long prior black real body.

23. The harami patterns are shown at 1, 3, and 4. I would not view signal 2 as a classic harami since this pattern should have an unusually long real body as the first candle of that pattern and, in this instance, the real body

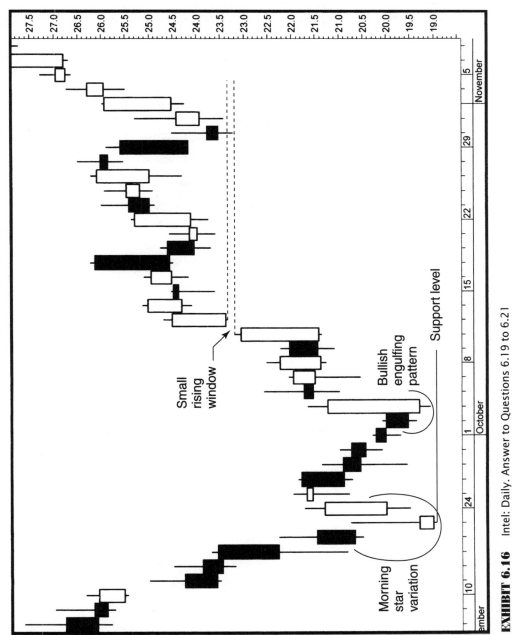

EXHIBIT 6.16 Intel: Daily. Answer to Questions 6.19 to 6.21

© Charts powered by MetaStock. Used by permission.

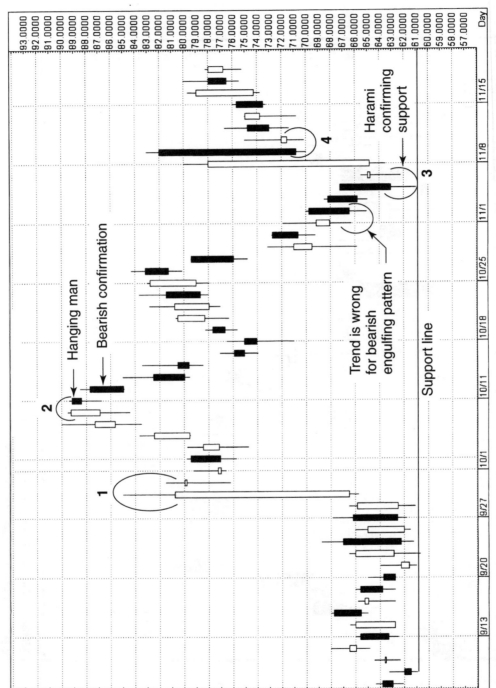

EXHIBIT 6.17 Amazon: Daily. Answers to Questions 6.22 to 6.24

© Aspen Graphics. Used by permission.

was not unusually long. With candlestick charting, just as with Western charting techniques, some subjectivity is involved in the analysis.

24. The two candle lines at C were especially significant because they formed a harami (as detailed in answer 23) and confirmed an important support area near 61.

25. The only hammer in this chart occurred on February 24. Let's go through each line (Exhibit 6.18). Line 1 is not hammer because it doesn't come after a downtrend. Line 2 isn't a hammer because the lower shadow wasn't long enough relative to the real body (the lower shadow should be at least twice the height of the real body). Line 3 meets all the criteria for a hammer. Specifically, the market is in a downtrend with the candlestick line with a long lower shadow (at least twice the height of the real body), little or no upper shadow, and a small real body at the top end of the trading range. Lines 4, 5, and 6 are not hammers. Although the shape of the candlestick lines are the same as a hammer, one of the criteria for a hammer is that must come after a downtrend (since it is a bottom reversal signal) and therefore we need a descending market to meet a necessary condition for hammer. Each of these lines did not come after a downtrend. This brings to the fore an important concept with candlesticks: It is not only the shape of the line that defines the pattern, but it's also the trend.

26. In Exhibit 6.18, line 1 is a doji. Lines 2 and 3 are shooting stars.

27. Although the first candle line on March 20 was a doji, there was also a rising window, which became a support area. Therefore, to confirm the potential bearish applications of the doji we have to wait for close under the bottom of the rising support line. This occurred later in the session on this intraday chart.

28. To confirm the negative implications of the doji we would need to see a close under the rising window's support area. This occurred at 14:00 on March 20 via a long black candle.

29. **h.** Signals 1 are shooting stars.

30. **b.** Signal 2 is a bullish harami.

31. **i.** Signal 3 is a hammer (it could also be considered a dragonfly doji).

32. **a.** Signal 4 is a bullish engulfing pattern.

33. **d.** Signal 5 is a falling window.

34. **e.** Signal 6 is a Southern doji (a doji that emerges during a decline).

35. **a.** Signal 7 is a bullish engulfing pattern.

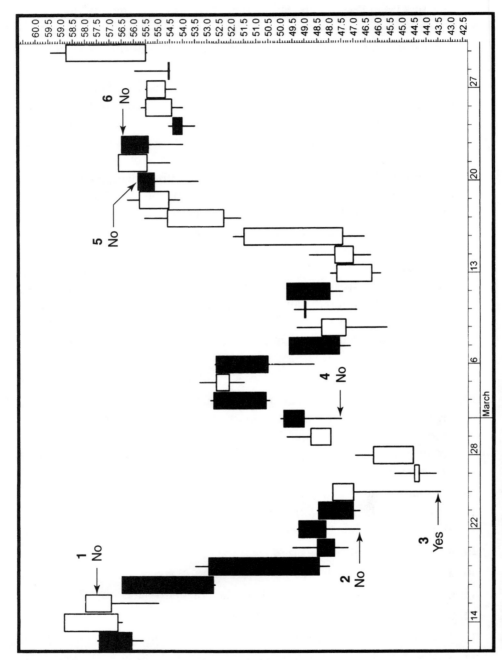

EXHIBIT 6.18 Wal-Mart: Daily. Answer to Question 6.25

© Charts powered by MetaStock. Used by permission.

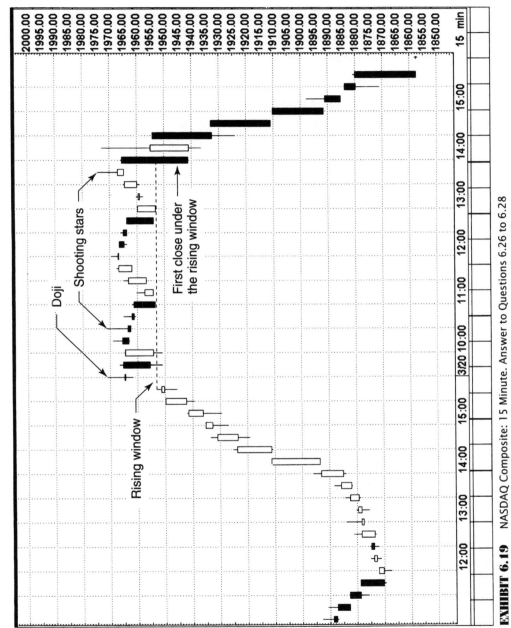

EXHIBIT 6.19 NASDAQ Composite: 15 Minute. Answer to Questions 6.26 to 6.28

© Aspen Graphics. Used by permission.

36. f. The three candle lines that form signal 8 make up a morning star.

37. g. Signal 9 is a Northern doji (a doji during an advance).

38. c. Signal 10 is a bearish harami (the second real body is so small it can also be considered a harami cross).

39. b. Signal 11 is a bullish harami.

40. i. Signal 12 is a hammer (also a dragonfly doji).

41. a. Signal 13 is a bullish engulfing pattern.

42. i. Signal 14 is a hammer.

Conclusion

There is a proverb: "Fish for me and I will eat for today, but teach me how to fish and I will eat the rest of my life." I hope this book has helped teach you to fish. By detailing the basic concepts of the candle charts and then having you test your skill with questions, real-world examples, and day-by-day analysis, I hope I have helped you down the road to candlestick analysis.

I invite you to sign up for our free biweekly educational e-newsletter. Each newsletter details a specific trading tool or technique using real-world examples. This is a perfect way to continue your candlestick education.

A Japanese Samurai general said, "Learning is the gate, not the house. You have to get to the gate before you go to the house." With this book I have taken you to the gate. There are many more techniques, concepts, and trading strategies that are beyond the scope of this book.

To learn all that our site has to offer and to sign up for this free e-newsletter please go to www.candlecharts.com. Following is a partial list of services and products designed to help you fully harness the power of candle charts:

- Video seminars
- Online seminars
- Public seminars
- Institutional on-site seminars
- Candlestick trading software
- Real-time candlestick recognition software
- Private coaching
- Advisory services

Visual Glossary of Candlestick Terms Used in This Book

The descriptions in this glossary give ideal versions of the patterns. Keep in mind that since there is some subjectivity, some less-than-perfect patterns can be valid signals. After each definition the following abbreviations are used to show market implications:

B Bullish
BR Bearish
LF Prior trend losing force
TC Trend change

Although the candlestick signals may convey bearishness or bullishness, they do not imply the market will reverse. The bearish candle signal means that the market has gone from up to neutral, or from down to neutral in the case of a bullish candle signal. Of course, whether one trades or not on the signal depends on many factors, one of the most important of which is the risk/reward of the trade.

Please note that since this book is a primer on candle charting techniques, not all candlestick patterns and terms are included in this glossary. For a complete glossary of all the candlestick patterns please visit our site at www.candlecharts.com.

belt-hold lines There are bullish and bearish belt holds (Exhibit G.1). A *bullish belt-hold* (B) is a tall white candlestick that opens on or near its low and closes well above the opening price. A *bearish belt-hold* (BR) is a long black candlestick that opens on or near its high and closes well off its open.

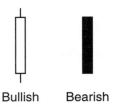

Bullish Bearish

EXHIBIT G.1 Belt-hold lines

candlestick charts Traditional Japanese charts whose individual lines look like candles (Exhibit G.2). Aso called candle charts. The candlestick line is made up of a real body and shadows. See *real body* and *shadows*.

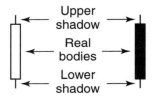

EXHIBIT G.2 Candlestick lines

counterattack lines A *bullish counterattack line* (B) occurs when a black candle in a downtrend is followed in the next session by the market gapping sharply lower on the opening and then closing unchanged from the prior session's close (Exhibit G.3). A *bearish counterattack line* (BR) occurs when a white candle in an uptrend is followed in the next session by the market gap-

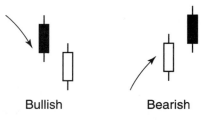

Bullish Bearish

EXHIBIT G.3 Counterattack lines

ping sharply higher on the open and then closing unchanged from the prior session's close.

dark cloud cover (BR)   In an uptrend a long white candlestick is followed by a black candlestick that opens above the prior white candlestick's high (or close) and then closes well into the white candlestick's real body—preferably more than halfway (Exhibit G.4).

EXHIBIT G.4   Dark cloud cover

doji (LF)   A session in which the open and close are the same, or almost the same (Exhibit G.5). There are different varieties of doji lines (see *gravestone, dragonfly,* and *long-legged doji*), depending on where the opening and closing are in relation to the entire range. *Northern doji* are doji that appear during a rally. *Southern doji* appear during declines.

EXHIBIT G.5   Doji

dragonfly doji (B)   A doji with a long lower shadow, in which the open, high, and close are at the session's high (Exhibit G.6).

EXHIBIT G.6   Dragonfly doji

engulfing patterns   A *bullish engulfing pattern* (B) is comprised of a large white real body that engulfs a small black real body in a downtrend (Exhibit G.7). A *bearish engulfing pattern* (BR) occurs when selling pressure overwhelms buying force, as reflected by a long black real body engulfing a small white real body in an uptrend.

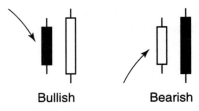

Bullish   Bearish

EXHIBIT G.7   Engulfing patterns

evening star (BR)   A pattern formed by three candle lines. The first is a tall white real body, and the second is a small real body (white or black), which gaps above the first real body to form a *star*. The third is a black candle that closes well into the first session's white real body (Exhibit G.8). If the middle portion of this pattern is a doji instead of a spinning top, it is an *evening doji star*.

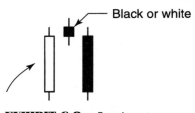

Black or white

EXHIBIT G.8   Evening star

falling window   See *windows*.

gravestone doji (BR)   A doji in which the opening and closing are at the low of the session (Exhibit G.9).

EXHIBIT G.9   Gravestone doji

hammer (B)   A small real body (white or black) at the top of the session's range and a very long lower shadow (with little or no upper shadow) that appears during a downtrend (Exhibit G.10). The lower shadow should be at least twice the height of the real body.

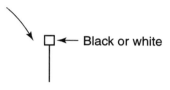

EXHIBIT G.10   Hammer

hanging man (BR)   The hanging man and the hammer are both the same type of candlestick line: a small real body, either white or black, with little or no upper shadow, at the top of the session's range, and having a very long lower shadow (Exhibit G.11). When the hanging man appears during an uptrend, it becomes a bearish hanging man. Because of the bullish long lower shadow, this pattern needs bearish confirmation by a close under the hanging man's real body.

EXHIBIT G.11   Hanging man

harami (TC)   A two-candlestick pattern in which a small real body holds within the prior session's unusually large real body (Exhibit G.12).

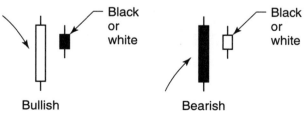

EXHIBIT G.12   Harami

high wave candle (TC)   A candle with a very long upper or lower shadow and a short real body (Exhibit G.13). If the real body is a doji instead of a small real body, it is a *long-legged doji*.

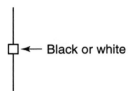

EXHIBIT G.13   High wave candlestick

morning star (B)   A pattern formed by three candlesticks (Exhibit G.14). The first is a long black real body. The second is a small real body (white or black), which gaps lower to form a star. The third is a white candlestick that closes well into the first session's black real body.

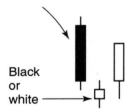

EXHIBIT G.14   Morning star

piercing pattern (B)   In a downtrend, a long black candlestick is followed by a gap lower during the next session (Exhibit G.15). This session finishes as a strong white candlestick that closes more than halfway into the prior black candlestick's real body.

EXHIBIT G.15   Piercing pattern

rising window   See *windows*.

real body   The rectangular part of the candlestick line. It is defined by the closing and opening prices of the session. When the close is higher than the open, the real body is white (or empty). A black (or filled-in) real body occurs when the close is lower than the opening (see Exhibit G.2).

shadows   The thin lines above and below the real body of the candlestick line. They represent the extremes of the session. The lower shadow is the line under the real body. The bottom of the lower shadow is the low of the session. The upper shadow is the line on top of the real body. The top of the upper shadow is the high of the session (see Exhibit G.2).

shooting star (BR)   A candle with a long upper shadow with little, or no lower shadow, and a small real body near the lows of the session that arises after an uptrend (Exhibit G.16).

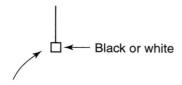

— Black or white

EXHIBIT G.16   Shooting star

spinning tops (TC)   The nickname for candle lines with small real bodies (Exhibit G.17).

EXHIBIT G.17   Spinning tops

three crows (BR)   Three relatively long consecutive black candles that close near or on their lows (Exhibit G.18).

EXHIBIT G.18   Three crows

three white or three advancing soldiers (B)   A group of three white candlesticks with consecutively higher closes, with each closing near the highs of the session (Exhibit G.19).

EXHIBIT G.19   Three advancing soldiers

tweezers top (BR) and **bottom** (B)   Tweezers occur when the same highs or lows are tested on back-to-back sessions. Ideally, the first candle should have a large real body and the second candle a small real body (Exhibit G.20).

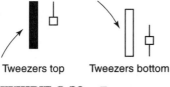

Tweezers top   Tweezers bottom

EXHIBIT G.20   Tweezers

window The same as a Western gap (Exhibit G.21). Windows are continuation patterns. When the market opens a window to the up side it is a *rising window* (B). If a window opens in a sell-off, it is a *falling window* (BR).

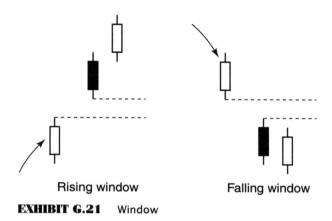

Rising window   Falling window

EXHIBIT G.21 Window

Index